ART MASTERS

# MICHELANGELO

GABRIELLA DI CAGNO

◆

ILLUSTRATED BY
SIMONE BONI & L.R. GALANTE

THE OLIVER PRESS, INC.
MINNEAPOLIS

# ♦ How to Use this Book

Produced by
*Donati-Giudici Associati, Firenze*
Original title
*Michelangelo*
Text
*Gabriella di Cagno*
Illustrations
*Simone Boni,*
*L.R. Galante,*
*Andrea Ricciardi,*
*Sergio*
Picture research
*Caroline Goddard*
Graphic design
*Oliviero Ciriaci*
Art direction
*Sebastiano Ranchetti*
Page design
*Laura Ottina Davis*
Editing
*Enza Fontana*
English translation
*Susan Ashley*
Editor, English-language edition
*Susan Ashley*
Cover design
*Icon Productions*

Original edition copyright © 1996
Donati Giudici Associati s.r.l.
Firenze, Italia

© 2008 by VoLo publisher srl,
Firenza, Italia

This edition © 2008 by
The Oliver Press, Inc.
5707 West 36th Street
Minneapolis, MN 55416
United States of America
www.oliverpress.com

Publisher Cataloging Information

Di Cagno, Gabriella
    Michelangelo / Gabriella Di
Cagno ; illustrated by Simone Boni & L.R.
Galante ; [English translation, Susan
Ashley].
    p. cm. – (Art masters)
    Includes bibliographical
references and index.
    Summary: With reproductions of
art masterpieces in full color, this book
examines the life and art of Michelangelo
and focuses on the cultural developments
of the era in which he lived.
    ISBN 978-1-934545-01-0
    1. Michelangelo Buonarroti,
1475-1564–Juvenile literature 2. Artists–
Italy–Biography–Juvenile literature
3. Art, Renaissance–Italy–Juvenile
literature [1. Michelangelo Buonarroti,
1475-1564 2. Artists] I. Ashley, Susan
II. Title III. Series
    2008
    709'.2–dc22
    [B]

ISBN 978-1-934545-01-0

Printed in Italy

11 10    4 3 2

Each double-page spread is a chapter in its own right, devoted to a key theme in the life and art of Michelangelo or the major artistic and cultural developments of his time. The text at the top of the left-hand page (1) introduces the theme. The text below (2) gives a chronological account of events in Michelangelo's life. The smaller text and illustrations on the spread expand on the central theme.

Some double-page spreads focus on major works by Michelangelo. The text in the left-hand column (1) gives a detailed description of the work. The text at the top (2) provides the context in which it was created, while the text below (3) offers a critical analysis of the work. The spread offers further examination of the work in the form of detailed close-ups and examples of how the work influenced other artists.

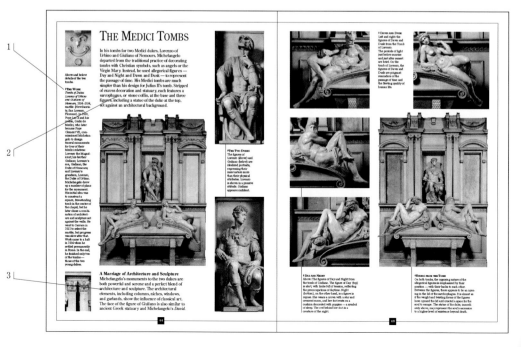

# CONTENTS

# CONTEMPORARIES

Michelangelo was recognized by his own contemporaries as one of the greatest artists of his time. He excelled at painting, sculpture, and architecture. Some of the most famous masterpieces of the Renaissance included his Sistine Chapel frescoes, the statue of *David*, and the great dome of St. Peter's. Possessing enormous talent, energy, and drive, he undertook most tasks single-handedly. He worked in Florence and Rome, the two centers of the Italian Renaissance, where he served powerful patrons, such as Lorenzo the Magnificent and Pope Julius II. They found in Michelangelo an artist who could express their ambitions through his brilliant works of art.

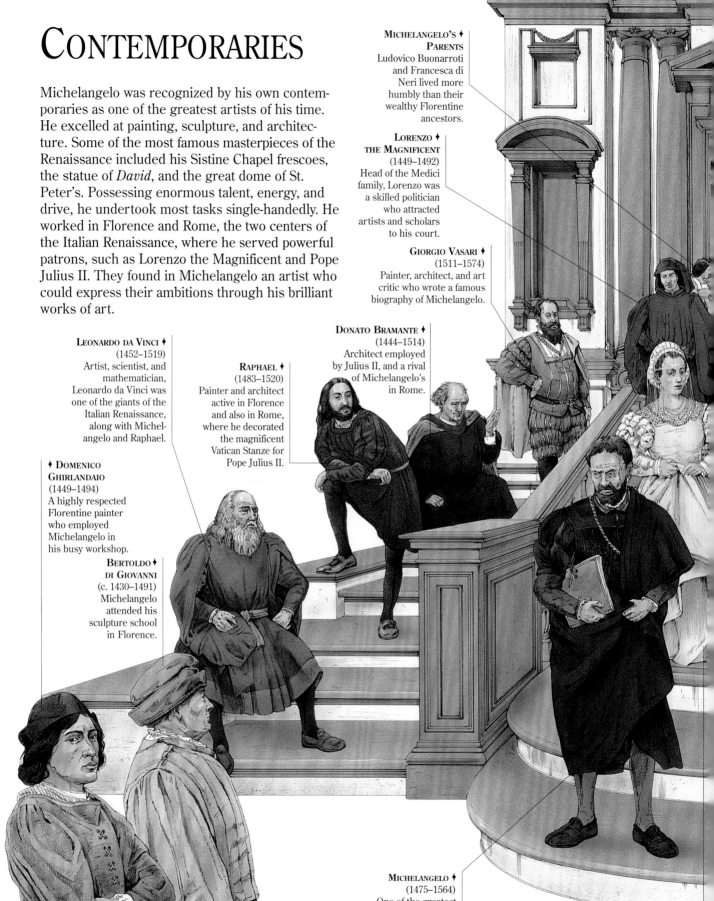

**MICHELANGELO'S ✦ PARENTS**
Ludovico Buonarroti and Francesca di Neri lived more humbly than their wealthy Florentine ancestors.

**LORENZO ✦ THE MAGNIFICENT**
(1449–1492)
Head of the Medici family, Lorenzo was a skilled politician who attracted artists and scholars to his court.

**GIORGIO VASARI ✦**
(1511–1574)
Painter, architect, and art critic who wrote a famous biography of Michelangelo.

**DONATO BRAMANTE ✦**
(1444–1514)
Architect employed by Julius II, and a rival of Michelangelo's in Rome.

**LEONARDO DA VINCI ✦**
(1452–1519)
Artist, scientist, and mathematician, Leonardo da Vinci was one of the giants of the Italian Renaissance, along with Michelangelo and Raphael.

**RAPHAEL ✦**
(1483–1520)
Painter and architect active in Florence and also in Rome, where he decorated the magnificent Vatican Stanze for Pope Julius II.

**✦ DOMENICO GHIRLANDAIO**
(1449–1494)
A highly respected Florentine painter who employed Michelangelo in his busy workshop.

**BERTOLDO ✦ DI GIOVANNI**
(c. 1430–1491)
Michelangelo attended his sculpture school in Florence.

**MICHELANGELO ✦**
(1475–1564)
One of the greatest artists of the sixteenth century, he was a stubborn character, brusque in manner and solitary by nature.

**VITTORIA COLONNA ✦**
(1490–1547)
A Roman noblewoman and poet, she became a close friend of Michelangelo.

✦**POPE JULIUS II**
(1443–1513)
A powerful ruler and
art patron, he
commissioned
Michelangelo to
paint the Sistine
Chapel ceiling.

✦**POPE LEO X**
(1475–1521)
A Medici, he hired
Michelangelo to
design a facade for
the Florentine church
of San Lorenzo.

✦**POPE CLEMENT VII**
(1478–1534)
Nephew of Lorenzo
the Magnificent, he
asked Michelangelo
to paint *The Last
Judgment* on the
end wall of the
Sistine Chapel.

**STONE CUTTERS** ✦
Stone cutters were
craftsmen skilled in
the cutting and
preparation of
marble and other
stone. Michelangelo
grew up among a
family of stone
cutters and, unlike
most of his
contemporaries,
never despised
manual work.

✦**POPE PAUL III**
(1468–1549)
The last pope to
employ Michelan-
gelo, he appointed
him chief architect
of St. Peter's.

✦**MARSILIO FICINO**
(1433–1499)
Philosopher whose
translations of Plato
into Latin had an
enormous impact on
the Renaissance.

✦**ANGELO POLIZIANO**
(1454–1494)
A scholar, poet, and
professor who tutored
the children of Lorenzo
the Magnificent.

✦**COSIMO I**
(1519–1574)
The first Grand
Duke of Tuscany,
he was a ruthless
politician and a
patron of the arts.

✦**ELEANORA
OF TOLEDO**
The daughter of the
Spanish viceroy of
Naples and wife
of Cosimo I. She
commissioned many
works of art for the
city of Florence.

✦**PICO DELLA
MIRANDOLA**
(1463–1494)
Philosopher and
scholar who lived
in Florence and
was a prominent
figure at the court
of Lorenzo the
Magnificent.

# SCULPTURE

Renaissance is a French word meaning "rebirth" and it refers to a rebirth of interest in ancient Greek and Roman art during the fifteenth and sixteenth centuries. The Renaissance began in Florence, a city in northern Italy, in the fifteenth century. The rediscovery of ancient works of art inspired Florentine artists to look at sculpture in a new way. During the Middle Ages, sculpture had focused on religious themes, and statues were stiff, elongated, and often placed up against a wall, as if they were part of the architecture. During the Renaissance, the human figure took on a new realism. Artists studied human proportions and represented people in natural poses. Figures were no longer represented from the front only, but were fully three-dimensional and free-standing, as they had been in ancient times.

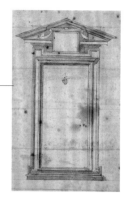

**STUDY FOR ✦ A DOORWAY** Michelangelo designed the elegant frame of this doorway in 1526. The stone cutters of Settignano were especially skilled in carving such details. (Casa Buonarroti, Florence).

**✦SAINT GEORGE** Donatello carved this figure in 1416–1420 for a niche in the outside wall of a building in Florence. The figure is realistic, with a natural stance and expression. (Museo del Bargello, Florence).

**✦THE STONE CUTTERS OF SETTIGNANO** Marble was a vital material during the Renaissance. Sculptures were carved out of large blocks of marble. It was also used to decorate the outside of important buildings. The village of Settignano, near Florence, was famous for its marble quarries. The area produced several talented sculptors and had a profound impact on Michelangelo. When he was a boy, Michelangelo lived in Settignano with a stone cutter and his wife. He became familiar with the tools and techniques of working in stone. When he expressed an interest in becoming a sculptor, however, his father was indignant. At the time, a sculptor was considered to be a craftsman, not an artist. That would soon change, but Michelangelo's father was opposed to his son's interest in pursing a "craft."

**✦CARVING CAPITALS** A stone cutter finishes the decorative capital, or top, of a column.

**MOLDINGS ✦** Stone cutters had to carve the decorative elements of moldings so they would fit together accurately.

**♦ SMALL SCULPTURES**
In the fifteenth century, wealthy Florentine families commissioned small sculptures to decorate their homes. An example is this *Madonna and Child* by Donatello, one of the most famous Florentine sculptors. (Louvre, Paris).

**♦ CUTTING THE STONE**
Stone cutters used large, specially designed equipment to cut the heavy stone.

**♦ FOUNTAIN**
This *Putto with Dolphin*, c. 1476, was designed for a fountain. Water sprayed out of the dolphin's mouth. It was designed by Florentine artist Andrea del Verrocchio, who influenced both Michelangelo and Leonardo da Vinci. (Palazzo Vecchio, Florence).

**♦ APOLLO**
The influence of classical sculpture is apparent in this small bronze *Apollo* by Bertoldo di Giovanni. Michelangelo attended his school in Florence. (Museo del Bargello, Florence).

**MICHELANGELO'S ♦ NURSE**
Michelangelo's mother was too ill to nurse him, so he was sent to live with a stone cutter and his wife.

## MICHELANGELO'S LIFE

Michelangelo Buonarroti was born in the village of Caprese, in the northern Italian region of Tuscany, on March 6, 1475. His mother, Francesca di Neri, was too ill to nurse him and sent him to live with a family of stone cutters in the nearby village of Settignano. His father, Ludovico Buonarroti, was a minor public official whose ancestors had held important posts in the Florentine government. Ludovico hoped to regain the family's former position in society and urged Michelangelo to become a businessman. When he discovered his son wanted to be a sculptor, he was furious.

# DRAWING

One of the factors that made Florentine artists stand out among their Renaissance contemporaries was their skill at drawing. For Florentines, draftsmanship was the foundation of all art, whether painting, sculpture, or architecture. Students in the workshops had to master drawing before moving on to other disciplines. Michelangelo was an apprentice in the workshop of Domenico Ghirlandaio, where he learned the technique of using pen and ink. Artists used drawings to do preliminary sketches for new paintings or sculptures. Drawings allowed them to study the proportions and positions of various figures or work on the composition as a whole. The growing importance of drawing also confirmed the changing status of the artist in society. More than a humble craftsman, an artist was a person of unique, creative talent.

**♦ A PORTRAIT**
Michelangelo drew this *Portrait of Andrea Quaratesi* in charcoal. Charcoal was generally used for preliminary sketches and studies because it made a soft line that was easy to erase. 1530–1540 (British Museum, London).

**PREPARING ♦ THE PAPER**
Before drawing, especially with a metal point, the paper was coated with a liquid containing the dust of animal bones and the desired pigment, or color. The coating made the paper strong and smooth.

**GHIRLANDAIO ♦**
The technique of pen-and-ink drawing was highly developed in Ghirlandaio's workshop. The drawing above is one of his studies for a fresco painting in the Florentine church of Santa Maria Novella. c. 1485 (Uffizi, Florence).

**DRAWING BY PEN ♦**
Renaissance artists made drawings using pen and ink. The pen was a quill, or feather, from a bird. For ink, artists sometimes used the ink of a cuttlefish. Cuttlefish are called *seppia* in Italian. The color of the dark ink they produce became known as sepia.

**♦ VERROCCHIO**
Verrocchio ran one of the busiest workshops in Florence. Leonardo da Vinci was one of his pupils. This is a metal point drawing by Verrocchio. The paper has been primed with a ground mixture of orange-pink pigments, a popular color at the time.

## CHARCOAL ✦

Charcoal for drawing was made from burnt sticks of wood. Because charcoal tends to smudge, artists fixed their work with gum arabic — a natural gum that, when dry, binds pigments to paper. Gum arabic comes from various trees in Africa.

## SANGUINE ✦

In the late fifteenth century, artists began using a chalk pencil called "sanguine" for drawings. The name refers to its blood-red color. Sanguine was made from chalk or clay containing iron oxide, which provided the red tone. Michelangelo used sanguine for this study of a human figure. 1508–1512 (British Library, London).

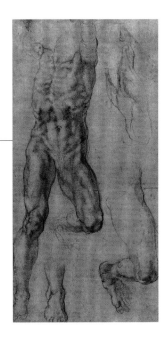

## ✦ DRAWING WITH A METAL POINT

Used by artists for hundreds of years, metal points were wooden pen-like instruments with a metal tip. The metal was usually lead or silver.

## ✦ COLORS

Although a type of tinted paper was available by the late fifteenth century, many artists preferred to prime paper using their own tints. They ground earth and minerals of various colors with a mortar and pestle, diluted the mixture with a liquid, and then spread it on the paper with a brush.

## MICHELANGELO'S LIFE

Michelangelo's mother died when he was six years old. The following year, his father sent him to a grammar school where he met some older students who were assistants in a painter's workshop. At the time, artists often hired assistants to help them complete their commissions. Artists' workshops were also schools where young students could learn from the masters. Michelangelo learned the rudiments of painting from his school companions. At age thirteen, he befriended a pupil of the renowned Florentine painter Domenico Ghirlandaio. Michelangelo's father strongly disapproved of his son's passion for art, but reluctantly allowed him to apprentice with Ghirlandaio — as long as the artist paid his son. This was unheard of at the time, but Michelangelo was so talented, Ghirlandaio agreed to pay him a wage.

# Painting

Giotto, a Florentine artist of the late thirteenth and early fourteenth centuries, was the first Italian painter to move away from the stiff, idealized figures of the Middle Ages to a more realistic style. His work inspired another Florentine, Tommaso Cassai, better known as Masaccio. Masaccio worked in the early fifteenth century and is considered the first master of Renaissance painting. His landscapes were natural and his figures were expressive and three-dimensional. Masaccio was also one of the first artists to apply the new scientific rules of perspective to painting. Michelangelo admired both of these early masters and studied and copied their works.

**♦ LEARNING FROM GIOTTO**
Renaissance painters in Florence were inspired by the work of fourteenth-century artists, particularly Giotto. Michelangelo's study of two male figures (above, left), c. 1490 (Louvre, Paris), is a copy of part of Giotto's fresco *The Ascension of St. John* (above, right), 1315–1320 (Santa Croce, Florence). This is Michelangelo's first known drawing. It shows how his study of Giotto and his classes in Ghirlandaio's workshop helped him depict human posture and the drapery of clothing.

**♦ LEARNING FROM MASACCIO**
Far left: Masaccio's *The Tribute Money*, c. 1425 (Brancacci Chapel, Florence); and near left: Michelangelo's copy of the figure of St. Peter, c. 1490 (Graphische Sammlungen, Munich). Both works appear three-dimensional.

**A SCHOLAR ♦**
St. Jerome translated the Bible from Greek into Latin in the fourth century AD. This painting shows him at his writing desk, surrounded by bookshelves. Antonello da Messina, *St. Jerome in his Study,* 1474. (National Gallery, London).

**LORENZO THE MAGNIFICENT ♦**
Lorenzo de Medici was the ruler of Florence from 1469 until his death in 1492. Known as Lorenzo the Magnificent to his contemporaries, he encouraged Florentines' growing interest in classical Greek and Roman culture. Lorenzo was a patron of philosophers and writers and a collector of books and classical works of art. He supported contemporary artists and welcomed them to his various residences. The political stability he achieved created an environment in which art could flourish. Right: a portrait of Lorenzo by Giorgio Vasari, 1488–1490 (Uffizi, Florence).

## MICHELANGELO'S LIFE

As an apprentice in Ghirlandaio's workshop, Michelangelo practiced drawing and learned the basics of fresco painting. He studied with great intensity and was soon good enough to correct the drawings of his fellow students. At the same time, he took an interest in statuary and went on his own to learn from the works of great Florentine sculptors, such as Donatello and Lorenzo Ghiberti. Rather than spend the usual three years as an apprentice in Ghirlandaio's workshop, he left after a year to apply himself to sculpture.

**♦ LORENZO'S ARTISTS**
In this fresco of 1636 by Francesco Furini, Lorenzo de Medici is surrounded by the artists he patronized. Michelangelo (on the right) is showing Lorenzo his sculpture of the head of a faun — the work which is said to have alerted Lorenzo to his great gifts. (Palazzo Pitti, Florence).

**THE LIFE OF ✦ ST. PETER**
On the left-hand wall of the Brancacci chapel, Masaccio painted *Stories from the Life of St. Peter*.

**✦ THE BRANCACCI CHAPEL**
The chapel, in the church of Santa Maria del Carmine, is named after Felice Brancacci, a Florentine ambassador who paid for the chapel to be decorated with frescoes.

**✦ PARADISE LOST**
On the right-hand wall of the Brancacci Chapel, Masaccio painted *The Expulsion of Adam and Eve from the Earthly Paradise*, c. 1425.
The bodies of the two figures above are reminiscent of classical sculpture and the works of contemporaries like Donatello. Their faces express intense emotion. These characteristics would appear in Michelangelo's work, particularly in his portrayal of the same scene on the ceiling of the Sistine Chapel in Rome.

**✦ ADAM AND EVE**
Next to Masaccio's frescoes in the Brancacci Chapel are scenes painted a year or so earlier by Masolino da Panicale, including *Adam and Eve before their Expulsion* (above), c. 1424. Compared to Masaccio's figures, those by Masolino are stiff and flat, with very little facial expression.

# IN LORENZO'S GARDEN

♦ **MARSILIO FICINO**
Marsilio translated the works of Plato, an ancient Greek philosopher, from Greek into Latin, and founded an important Platonic academy in Florence. This bust of Marsilio was made by Andrea Ferrucci in 1522. (Florence Cathedral).

Fifteenth-century Florence was the center of a renewed interest in classical culture. Perhaps no one was more enthusiastic about this development than the city's ruler, Lorenzo de Medici, known as Lorenzo the Magnificent. He surrounded himself with the most brilliant scholars, writers, and artists of the day, often inviting them to live in his home. He hired noted philosophers to tutor his children. Like other wealthy rulers of his time, he collected ancient Greek and Roman art. He filled his garden with classical statues and invited Florentine sculptor Bertoldo di Giovanni to use the garden as a training ground for sculptors. Michelangelo became a pupil at the school.

♦ **A CAMEO**
In this portrait by Florentine painter Sandro Botticelli, the woman wears a cameo from Lorenzo the Magnificent's collection. Renaissance cameos often featured scenes from Greek mythology. *Portrait of a Young Woman*, 1483 (Kunstinstitut Gemaldegalerie, Frankfurt).

♦ **PLATO AND NEOPLATONISM**
The study of classical culture led to a renewed interest in the philosopher Plato (427–347 BC). His ideas were compatible with Christian teaching, particularly regarding creation, the existence of one God, and the immortality of the soul. The resulting philosophy, based on Plato's teachings, was called Neoplatonism and it dominated fifteenth-century Florentine thought. Artists drew inspiration from parables invented by Plato. In his parable of the chariot, for example, the chariot is a symbol of the human soul, drawn by two horses — passion and reason. The driver is the human mind, whose task is to keep those opposing forces in balance. The parable is depicted above in a bronze medallion attributed to Bertoldo, 1440. (Museo del Bargello, Florence).

**PLANTS ♦**
Renaissance gardens were home to rare species, as well as more common plants. Cypress trees were favorite evergreens.

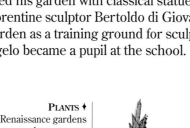

**LORENZO ♦ THE MAGNIFICENT**
Lorenzo took great pride in his collection of classical statues. People came to his garden to see them and to visit his school.

## MICHELANGELO'S LIFE
After a year in Ghirlandaio's workshop, Michelangelo persuaded his father to let him study sculpture. He enrolled in the school run by Bertoldo di Giovanni, who had been a pupil of the Florentine sculptor Donatello. Classes were held in Lorenzo's garden. Lorenzo was impressed by Michelangelo's talent and took a great interest in him, even inviting him to live in his home. Lorenzo treated Michelangelo like a son. Because of his close ties to the Medici, Michelangelo lived in a cultured, stimulating environment, and was in close contact with the most celebrated thinkers of the day.

♦ **LORENZO'S CITY**
This detail from an illustration in a fifteenth-century book shows Florence at the time of Lorenzo's youth. In the center, on the left, is the Florence Cathedral with its great dome. Next to it is the Baptistry of St. John, and beyond that the Palazzo Vecchio, the seat of Florentine government. (From *Storia fiorentina* by Poggio Bracciolini, Vatican Library, Rome).

♦ **STUDENTS AT WORK**
The students worked under the shelter of an arcade. They were inspired by Lorenzo's collection of ancient statues in the garden.

♦ **THE FAUN**
While still a boy, Michelangelo carved the head of a faun, a mythological creature that was half-man, half-goat. This particular piece is said to have made Lorenzo aware of Michelangelo's talent and potential.

# BATTLE OF THE CENTAURS

Above and below: details from *The Battle of the Centaurs.*

Renaissance artists were drawn to mythological subjects. In Greek mythology, centaurs were creatures with the upper body of a man and the lower body of a horse. They were brutish in character and symbolic of the uncivilized, animal side of human nature. Michelangelo took his subject for the sculpture below from a myth originating in Thessaly, Greece. In the story, the centaurs are invited to the wedding feast of a peace-loving people known as the Lapiths. The centaurs, unused to drinking wine, become drunk and out of control and threaten the Lapiths. A battle ensues, in which the centaurs lose and are banished from Thessaly.

♦**A CLASSICAL MODEL**
Lorenzo the Magnificent's collection of antiquities included this ancient cameo with a centaur, from the second century AD. (Museo Nazionale, Naples).

♦**THE WORK**
*The Battle of the Centaurs,* 1492, marble relief, 33 x 36 inches (84.5 x 90.5 cm) (Casa Buonarroti, Florence). Michelangelo finished this work in 1492, shortly before the death of Lorenzo de Medici. It was the last work the young artist completed for his patron. The Florentine scholar Angelo Poliziano may have suggested the subject to Michelangelo, which symbolizes the victory of human reason (the Lapiths) over brute force (the centaurs). Such themes were common on ancient sarcophagi, or stone coffins. Of all the works of his youth, this is the only one in which Michelangelo did not use a bow drill. A bow drill was an instrument used for carving delicate objects and fine details, such as locks of hair or the folds of drapery. Renaissance sculptors used a variety of tools. Michelangelo used a chisel to give the background figures a rough finish. Rasps, or flat metal files, were often used for final shaping.

## MICHELANGELO'S CENTAURS
*The Battle of the Centaurs* is a relief sculpture, in which shallow figures are carved on a flat surface. The work is full of energy with its mass of tangled bodies. Michelangelo created the illusion of depth by making the figures in the foreground smooth and those in the background rough. The contrast between the deep shadows and the highlights of the polished figures also adds depth. This was one of Michelangelo's first sculptures, and one he later considered to be the best of his early works.

♦**CIRCULAR RELIEFS**
The courtyard of Lorenzo's palace featured circular reliefs like this fifteenth-century relief of a centaur. The designs were often reproductions of cameos in Lorenzo's collection.

♦ **BERTOLDO DI GIOVANNI**
This relief carving by Michelangelo's teacher was undoubtedly inspired by a classical piece of sculpture. Its crowded figures on a flat plane are similar to designs found on Roman sarcophagi. *Battle Scene*, bronze relief, mid-fifteenth century. (Museo del Bargello, Florence).

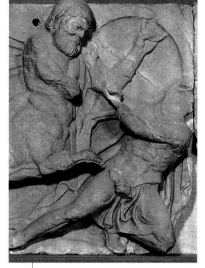

♦ **A ROMAN RELIEF**
Renaissance artists admired ancient reliefs. This carving from the third century AD was created for a Roman sarcophagus. It may have inspired Bertoldo's *Battle Scene* at the top of this page. (Museo delle Terme, Rome).

♦ **PAINTING OF A BATTLE**
*The Battle of Lapiths and Centaurs* by the Florentine artist Piero di Cosimo (1457–1521) is a painting based on the same story as Michelangelo's sculpture. Piero di Cosimo's style was highly detailed. Here, the details extend to the background landscape. (National Gallery, London).

♦ **A GREEK FRIEZE**
A centaur is the attacker in this battle scene. This detail is from the frieze of a Greek temple. A frieze is a horizontal band above the columns of a temple. It was usually decorated with carvings. (British Museum, London).

# SAVONAROLA

When the Dominican friar Girolamo Savonarola arrived in Florence in 1481, he was welcomed by Lorenzo de Medici. As time went on, however, Savonarola's preaching became increasingly zealous. He railed against church corruption and denounced material wealth. The Medicis and the pope became targets of his moral crusade. When the French king Charles VIII invaded Florence in 1494, the Medici were expelled and Savonarola became the spiritual leader of the city. He preached political as well as religious reform and helped introduce a republican form of government. His austere policies and excommunication by the pope, however, eventually turned the people of Florence against him. In 1498, he was burned at the stake.

**✦ SAVONAROLA**
Girolamo Savonarola (1452–1498) opposed the corruption of the Catholic Church and denounced worldly vanities.
*Portrait of Savonarola* by Fra Bartolomeo, early sixteenth century. (Museo di San Marco, Florence).

**✦ THE MONASTERY OF SAN MARCO**
During his years in Florence, Savonarola lived and preached at the monastery of San Marco. The complex included a church and a residence for the monks. The monks would retire to small rooms called cells to sleep or pray on their own. The cell walls were decorated with frescoes by Fra Angelico (c. 1395–1455) portraying scenes from the life of Christ.

**✦ CHARLES VIII**
In 1494, the French king Charles VIII and his army crossed into the Italian peninsula to take the kingdom of Naples. When Charles reached Florence on his way south, he entered the city triumphantly and occupied it for a short time. Below: Francesco Granacci, *Charles VIII Entering Florence,* early sixteenth century. (Uffizi, Florence).

**CLOISTER ✦**
The cloister was a central courtyard where the monks exercised. The cloister was surrounded by a row of columns, called a colonnade.

**CHAPTER HOUSE ✦**
The meeting room in a monastery was called a chapter house. It had to be large enough to hold all of the monks.

## ✦ THE CHURCH
Monks could enter the church directly from the cloister, without having to leave the complex and be exposed to the world outside.

## DEFENDING FLORENCE ✦
Charles VIII of France threatened to destroy Florence, claiming that the city owed him a sum of money. Pier Capponi, who led the defense of Florence against the French, defied Charles by tearing up the disputed document. The episode is recorded in this fresco by Bernardino Poccetti, 1583–1586. (Palazzo Capponi, Florence).

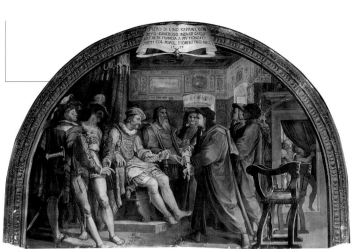

## ✦ THE LIBRARY
Here, in addition to studying, the monks made copies of ancient manuscripts, which they illuminated with beautiful miniature illustrations.

## ✦ SAVONAROLA'S END
Florentines eventually turned against Savonarola. He was accused of heresy, tortured until he confessed, and burned at the stake. Below: *The Burning of Savonarola in the Piazza della Signoria*, 1498. (Museo di San Marco, Florence).

## ✦ GUEST QUARTERS
Rooms on the ground floor were set aside for travelers seeking hospitality.

## ✦ PIERO II DE MEDICI
Piero, son and successor of Lorenzo de Medici, was weak and lacked the skills needed to govern Florence. When Charles VIII and his army entered the city, Piero put up no resistance. Bronzino, *Portrait of Piero II*, 1553. (Uffizi, Florence).

## MICHELANGELO'S LIFE
Michelangelo was seventeen when his benefactor Lorenzo de Medici died in 1492. He returned to his father's house, but was unhappy there. He continued to work alone, carving in stone and traveling to the Florentine monastery of Santo Spirito to study anatomy. The monks there allowed him to dissect the corpses coming from the monastery's hospital. At this time, Michelangelo became sensitive to spiritual matters and his faith was deepened by attending the church of San Marco, where he heard the preaching of Girolamo Savonarola. Ultimately, concerned by the worsening political situation in Florence and his difficult personal circumstances, Michelangelo left the city. He stayed for a time in Venice, then went to Bologna. In Bologna, he met some of the leading citizens, who introduced him to other artists and obtained commissions for him.

# ARCHITECTURE

Like painting and sculpture, Renaissance architecture found its inspiration in antiquity. Architects revived elements of ancient Greek and Roman temples, including columns, arches, and domes, and used them to decorate their buildings. Artists like Brunelleschi studied the mathematical dimensions of ancient structures and used them to construct buildings of harmonious proportions. Talented architects never lacked employment during the Renaissance. A grand structure could express wealth and power, and popes and princes tried to outdo one another in commissioning magnificent palaces, churches, and civic buildings.

**♦ FILIPPO BRUNELLESCHI**
A Florentine architect and sculptor, Brunelleschi (1377–1446) is considered the father of Renaissance architecture. A self-taught artist, he studied classical buildings to learn the secrets of their construction. He was also fascinated by mathematics, and formulated rules of perspective that were used by Renaissance painters. His greatest achievement was designing the great dome of the Florence Cathedral, 1420–1436 (above).

**♦ THE PAZZI CHAPEL**
In this early example of Renaissance architecture, 1430, Filippo Brunelleschi combined classical columns and arches.

**♦ PALAZZO RUCELLAI**
Alberti drew inspiration from classical architecture in designing this private residence for the Rucellai family, who were wealthy Florentine merchants.

**PIENZA ♦**
In 1459, Pope Pius II commissioned Bernardo Rossellino, an architect from Settignano and pupil of Alberti, to rebuild his hometown of Pienza according to Renaissance principles. The architect completed a new piazza and the buildings surrounding it, including the cathedral and the Palazzo Piccolomini (right).

**♦ LEON BATTISTA ALBERTI**
Born in Genoa, Alberti (1404–1472) was an architect, author, poet, and philosopher. He came to Florence in 1434 and quickly grasped the importance of the ideas introduced by Brunelleschi, Donatello, and Masaccio. He wrote theoretical works on painting and architecture. His own creations included the Tempio Malatestiano in Rimini, Sant'Andrea in Mantua, the Palazzo Rucellai in Florence, and the facade of another Florentine structure, the church of Santa Maria Novella (above), 1456–1470.

## MICHELANGELO'S LIFE
Michelangelo stayed in Bologna for about a year, and then returned to Florence. Upon his return, he carved a statue of a *Sleeping Cupid*. It was eventually sold for a high price to a Roman cardinal, Raffaele Riario. At the time, there was a brisk market in Rome for antiquities. Michelangelo's statue had been buried for a while to make it look old, and the cardinal thought he was buying a genuine piece of classical art. When he discovered he had been duped, he demanded his money back. At the same time, he was so impressed by the young sculptor's skill that he wanted to be his patron in Rome. Michelangelo arrived in Rome in June 1496. He stayed in the city for several years, studying classical works and completing two of his most famous sculptures: *Bacchus* and the *Pietà*.

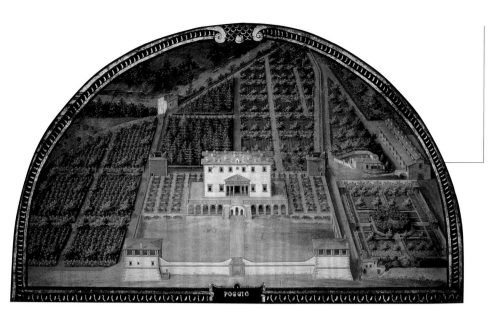

**♦ A MEDICI VILLA**
This painting from the late sixteenth century shows one of the Medici family's summer residences outside Florence. A fine example of Renaissance architecture, the villa was acquired by Lorenzo the Magnificent and rebuilt in 1480–1485 to a design by Giuliano da Sangallo, Lorenzo's preferred architect. The villa was surrounded by formal gardens. (Museo di Firenze, Florence).

**♦ BERNARDO ROSSELLINO**
A pupil of Alberti, Rossellino (1409–1464) was active as an architect in Rome and Tuscany. The commission that brought him the most fame, however, was designing the tomb of Leonardo Bruni, 1446–1450, (above) in the Florentine church of Santa Croce. The tomb, set against a wall, is surrounded by classical architectural elements. It set the standard for Renaissance tomb design.

**♦ NICCOLÒ TRIBOLO**
Tribolo was a Florentine sculptor in the service of the Medici. He became known for his garden designs. He created the statue above (Museo del Bargello, Florence) for a fountain in the garden of the Medici villa at Castello. The influence of Greek and Roman art is apparent in the design of Renaissance gardens and the statues and fountains that were made for them.

**♦ DONATO BRAMANTE**
Originally from Urbino, Bramante moved to Milan in 1474, where he received important commissions from Duke Ludovico Sforza. One was the building of Santa Maria delle Grazie, which houses Leonardo da Vinci's fresco *The Last Supper*. He later moved to Rome, where Pope Julius II commissioned him to rebuild St. Peter's Basilica.

Above: The plan for the circular Tempietto, a building in Rome. In designing this small structure, Bramante was inspired by the symmetry found in classical temples.

**♦ PALAZZO PICCOLOMINI**
The style of this Renaissance palace in Pienza resembles the Palazzo Rucellai in Florence. Alberti and Rossellino collaborated on both.

♦ **THE WORK**
*Bacchus*, 1496–1497, marble, 80 inches high (203 cm), including the base (Museo del Bargello, Florence). In late June 1496, Michelangelo made his first journey to Rome, where he was received by Cardinal Raffaele Riario, a collector of antiquities. The cardinal commissioned a statue of Bacchus for his garden. Michelangelo began working on it in July and completed it the following year. Slightly taller than life-size, it was his first large-scale work. The cardinal ultimately refused the statue and the work was bought by Jacopo Galli, the cardinal's banker, who placed it in his own garden. In 1570, the work was sold to a member of the Medici family. Later, it was acquired by the Uffizi Gallery in Florence, where it was placed alongside other classical statues. In 1871, the statue was transferred to the Museo del Bargello in Florence, which houses a large collection of Renaissance sculpture. There, among both Renaissance and modern works, its classical inspiration is all the more striking.

# BACCHUS

Bacchus, the Roman god of wine (known as Dionysus in Greek mythology), was a popular subject with artists of the sixteenth century. He was usually represented with a bunch of grapes and a staff wreathed with vine leaves and ivy. Celebrations in honor of Bacchus were called Bacchanalia. In ancient times, only women were allowed to attend these festivals. Other followers of the god included the satyrs, who were half-human and half-animal. Michelangelo created a statue of Bacchus in 1497. In his work, the god of wine seems a bit unsteady on his feet. A satyr appears behind him.

♦ **SANSOVINO**
Florentine sculptor Jacopo Sansovino carved a statue of *Bacchus and a Satyr* for the garden of a wealthy patron. It eventually found its way into the Medici collection, and is now on display at the Museo del Bargello in Florence, next to Michelangelo's statue of *Bacchus*.

## MICHELANGELO'S BACCHUS
Michelangelo first came into contact with classical sculpture at the home of Lorenzo the Magnificent. In Rome, he was able to deepen his knowledge by studying the Greek and Roman works collected by his patrons. His *Bacchus* shows the influence of ancient Greek sculpture with its relaxed pose and natural gaze. Like classical statues, it was intended to be viewed from every angle. The garden in which it was originally located was an ideal setting.

♦ **AT THE UFFIZI**
In a catalog from 1750, showing the Uffizi Gallery's collection of works, Michelangelo's *Bacchus* is shown in the eastern corridor of the museum, beneath a *Portrait of Eleanora of Toledo* and next to an antique bust.

**A ROMAN BACCHUS** ♦
In Rome, there was no lack of classical statues in the private collections of popes and wealthy citizens. (Vatican Museums, Rome).

♦ **ANDREA MANTEGNA**
This engraving by Mantegna, finished shortly before Michelangelo's statue, shows the festival of Bacchus and his worshippers exactly as described in artists' manuals of the time. *Bacchanalia with Wine Vat*, 1470–1490. (Uffizi, Florence).

**CLASSICAL INSPIRATION** ♦
Michelangelo may have been inspired by ancient works similar to this *Bacchus with Satyr*. (Vatican Museums, Rome).

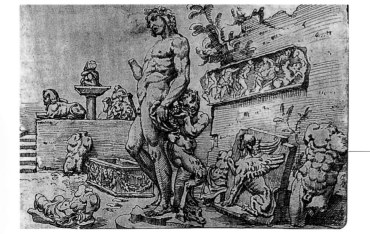

♦ **IN ROME**
Roman banker Jacopo Galli set Michelangelo's *Bacchus* in his garden, alongside his collection of other statues. This drawing by Martin van Heemsckerck shows the statue in Galli's collection. 1533 (Kupferstich-kabinett, Berlin).

# THE REPUBLIC

At the beginning of the fifteenth century, Florence was a republic. Unlike many other Italian states, its ruler was elected by representatives of the city's various neighborhoods and guilds. During the decades that followed, however, control of the city was firmly in the hands of the Medici dynasty. In 1494, after the flight of the Medici and the death of Savonarola, Florence experienced another period of republican government. It was threatened from without by hostile Italian and foreign powers, and from within by citizens still loyal to the Medici. To guarantee stability, Pier Soderini was elected head of state for life in 1502. The new government behaved like other Renaissance courts in commissioning prestigious projects, including the hiring of Michelangelo to produce the statue of *David*.

**DAVID ✦**
Michelangelo's statue was so large that a wall in the workshop where it was carved had to be demolished before it could be moved to its new site.

**DA VINCI'S ENVY ✦**
Leonardo da Vinci was among the crowd in the Piazza della Signoria the day the statue was unveiled. He and Michelangelo were artistic rivals. Da Vinci was envious of Michelangelo's prestigious commission.

**✦ MOVING THE STATUE**
It took forty men four days to move the huge statue from Michelangelo's workshop to the Piazza della Signoria.

♦ THE RIGHT PLACE
A committee of Florentines voted to decide where to place the statue. Some thought it should stand outside the city's cathedral. In the end, the statue was brought to the Piazza della Signoria and placed in front of the Palazzo Vecchio, the Florentine seat of government.

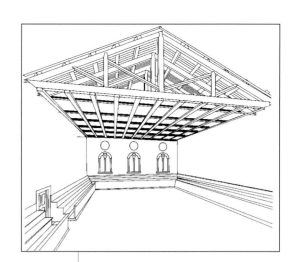

♦ THE "ROOM OF THE FIVE HUNDRED"
When the republic was re-established in 1494, a chamber was built in the Palazzo Vecchio for meetings of the Grand Council, which governed the city. The room had to be large enough to accommodate 500 people — the number of council members. An illustration of the room is shown above. Decoration of the Council Chamber was entrusted to the greatest Florentine artists of the day: Leonardo da Vinci and Michelangelo. Each was assigned to paint one wall of the long room.

MACHIAVELLI ♦
(1469–1527)
Niccolò Machiavelli served the Florentine Republic as a diplomat and military strategist. He is most famous for his political treatises, which were based on his experiences of the turbulent politics of Renaissance Italy. Late-fifteenth-century bust of Machiavelli (Museo del Bargello, Florence).

## MICHELANGELO'S LIFE

Michelangelo returned to Florence in the spring of 1501. Having no work to do, he pursued his anatomical studies at Santo Spirito and almost got into serious trouble for dissecting the corpse of an important Florentine citizen. In August, city officials approached him about carving an enormous block of marble. From this block, Michelangelo created his famous statue of *David*. The finished work was a great public success and it established his reputation once and for all. In 1504, Pier Soderini, the newly elected leader of Florence, asked Michelangelo to decorate one wall of the new Council Chamber in the Palazzo Vecchio, while his rival, Leonardo da Vinci, was to work on the other.

♦ **DETAILS**
Above and below:
*David*, details.

# DAVID

The story of David and Goliath was frequently portrayed in Renaissance art. In the biblical story, David, a shepherd boy, takes up the challenge of single combat against Goliath, the most terrifying Philistine warrior. Armed only with a sling and a few stones, David confronts Goliath. He strikes him with a single stone and the giant warrior falls to the ground, defeated. At the time Michelangelo presented his statue to the city, Florence was threatened by enemies on all sides. The figure of *David* took on political significance, representing the strength and freedom of the republic. Unlike other statues of David, Michelangelo's emphasized his subject's courage, depicting David at the tense moment before battle, rather than in relaxed pose afterward.

♦ **DETAILS**
Above and below:
*David*, details.

♦ **THE WORK**
*David*, marble, 1501–1504, height 17 feet (517 cm) (Galleria dell'Accademia, Florence). In August 1501, shortly after the proclamation of the new republic, the cathedral works department of Florence entrusted Michelangelo with a huge block of marble, nicknamed "the giant," from which he was to create a statue of David, a heroic character from the Old Testament of the Bible. A number of artists had already tried their hand at it, but the marble remained uncarved after twenty-five years. Michelangelo finished the statue in 1504. It was placed in the city's main square, the Piazza della Signoria, in front of the Palazzo Vecchio, the city's town hall. Given its location and colossal size, *David* soon became a powerful symbol of the city. The statue remained in the Piazza della Signoria for over 350 years. In 1873, it was moved, using complex machinery, to the Galleria dell'Accademia, a museum in Florence. A replica of the statue now stands in the square.

♦ **HERCULES**
This small Renaissance bronze, 1470–1475, may have been a model for Michelangelo's *David*. The statue portrays Hercules, a mythical hero celebrated for his great strength. Michelangelo used a similar pose to express the strength of David.

## MICHELANGELO'S DAVID

Michelangelo carved his enormous statue from a single block of marble. Over the course of three years, he gradually removed material from the front of the block to "release" the hidden form within. Like his statue of *Bacchus*, Michelangelo's *David* shows the influence of classical sculpture, particularly in the figure's stance. Most of the weight is on one leg. This balanced, but asymmetrical position, known as *contrapposto*, was common in ancient Greek statues. Michelangelo used it in many of his figures, in both sculpture and painting.

**♦ PRELIMINARY STUDY**
In the margin of this sketch for David's arm, Michelangelo wrote, "David with his sling and me with my bow." The artist was drawing a parallel between the weapon David used and his own bow drill, a tool commonly used by sculptors of the time. 1501–1504 (Louvre, Paris).

**♦ VERROCCHIO'S DAVID**
Andrea del Verrocchio, a Florentine artist with whom Leonardo da Vinci studied, created this elegant bronze statue of *David*. The work was commissioned by the Medici before 1476 and displayed inside the Palazzo Vecchio. Today, the statue is kept in the Museo del Bargello in Florence.

**♦ THE PIAZZA DELLA SIGNORIA**
This painting shows Michelangelo's *David* in its original site in the Piazza della Signoria. Giorgio Vasari, *The Arrival of Pope Leo X in Florence*, 1555–1562. (Palazzo Vecchio, Florence).

**DONATELLO'S DAVID ♦**
This bronze *David* by Donatello (c. 1430–1433) depicts the young hero in a reflective mood after his triumph. The figure is modeled according to classical rules of beauty. (Museo del Bargello, Florence).

# UNFINISHED WORKS

A number of Michelangelo's sculptures were never finished. During the Renaissance, talented artists were much in demand and often worked on several jobs simultaneously. Many hired assistants to help them, but Michelangelo preferred to work alone. This may explain the incomplete state of some of his pieces. Figures are still partially encased in their marble blocks, and instead of a smooth finish, the artist's deep chisel marks are plainly visible. These unfinished works are fascinating because they reveal Michelangelo's method of working.

✦ **FORM AND MATTER**
Michelangelo, *Atlas,* detail, 1513–1520. (Galleria dell'Accademia, Florence).

✦ **A ROUGH FINISH**
Some of Michelangelo's sculptures are more finished than others. In the works of his youth, such as the Vatican *Pietà*, he made extensive use of the bow drill. This tool enabled him to render fine details, such as hair, eyes, and other features. The finished carving would then be rubbed with abrasives to achieve a highly polished appearance. His later pieces were not always finished to this degree. The surface of the marble is heavily textured, showing the sharp cuts made by his claw chisel. This is especially apparent in works such as the four *Slaves.* The figures appear to be imprisoned in the marble and struggling to break free. In this sense, they represent Michelangelo's view of the sculptor's job, which is to "liberate" figures from the stone. Looking at the unfinished works on these pages, one can see his process — from the early, roughest cuts, to the more fully formed features that project from the block, to the final, polished statue. In their own way, his unfinished works are as powerful and emotional as his finished pieces.

✦ **MEDICI MADONNA**
This *Madonna and Child* is an example of a figure left unfinished. It stands above a Medici tomb in the church of San Lorenzo, but may have been carved originally for Julius II's tomb, c. 1521. (New Sacristy, San Lorenzo, Florence).

**POLISHED PIETÀ** ✦
Michelangelo's *Pietà* in the Vatican is his most carefully finished work. Every detail is painstakingly rendered and the surface is highly polished, 1498–1499. (St. Peter's, Rome).

✦ **RONDANINI PIETÀ**
The *Rondanini Pieta,* 1552–1564, was left unfinished at the time of Michelangelo's death. The basic shapes are roughed out and the artist's chisel marks are clearly visible (Castello Sforzesco, Milan).

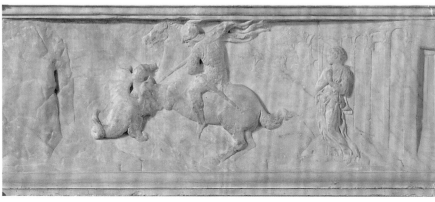

✦ **DONATELLO'S LOW RELIEF**
In this bas-relief on the base of Donatello's statue of *St. George,* the rough background is less sharply defined than the foreground to give a sense of depth, 1416–1420. (Museo del Bargello, Florence).

**✦ SLAVES**
Michelangelo carved the four marble statues on this page for the tomb of Pope Julius II. The design of the tomb changed many times over the years and the statues ultimately were not needed. They are known as "slaves" or "prisoners" because they communicate a sense of being imprisoned in their blocks of marble. Left: *Bearded Slave,* 1513–1520. (Galleria dell'Accademia, Florence).

**✦ THE YOUNG SLAVE**
Some scholars believe that the unfinished state of Michelangelo's four *Slaves* was intentional and that their attempts to break free of the marble are symbolic of human struggles.

**✦ ATLAS**
In the figure of *Atlas,* two sides of the original square block of marble are still visible.

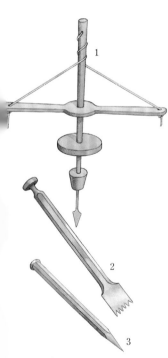

**✦ TOOLS**
Some of the tools Michelangelo used for his *Slaves* were:
(1) a bow drill
(2) a claw chisel
(3) a punch, or pointed chisel.

**✦ THE AWAKENING SLAVE**
Michelangelo shaped the marble block with a claw chisel, working his way through the stone layer by layer.

## MICHELANGELO'S LIFE

The commission to paint a fresco on the wall of Florence's Council Chamber was both prestigious and challenging. Michelangelo was asked to depict the victorious *Battle of Cascina* on one side of the room, while his rival, Leonardo da Vinci, was to paint the *Battle of Anghiari* on the opposite wall. Relations between the two men were not warm, and the commission itself took on aspects of a battle. Leonardo was in his early fifties and a celebrity, having just finished his *Mona Lisa.* Michelangelo was only twenty-nine, yet his own masterpiece, *David,* stood just outside the building. Unfortunately, the outcome of the artistic battle is unknown. Leonardo's work was painted over later and Michelangelo's never got past the drawing stage.

# Classical Rome

The discovery of classical statuary in the fifteenth century caused great excitement throughout Italy. Most of the statues were in Rome, where they had lain buried and forgotten during the Middle Ages. Their unearthing caused Rome to become a leading destination of scholars and art collectors. The city was also a magnet for artists seeking direct contact with classical culture, as well as something less noble — lucrative commissions. In Rome, the popes were the great art patrons. During the sixteenth century, they commissioned some of the greatest masterpieces in painting, sculpture, and architecture. They were also avid collectors of antiquities. To house his collection, Pope Julius II created the Belvedere Courtyard in the Vatican. It was Rome's first open-air sculpture museum.

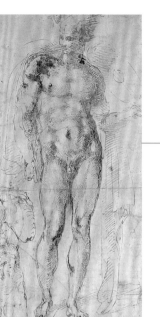

♦ **A STUDY BY MICHELANGELO**
Like most of his contemporaries, Michelangelo was fascinated by the sculptures housed at the Vatican. He made studies of them, including this drawing.

**THE BELVEDERE COURTYARD ♦**
It was Pope Julius II's idea to establish a museum of statuary in the Belvedere Courtyard of the Vatican. In 1505, he asked Donato Bramante to create a design that would link the courtyard and the Vatican Palace. Bramante's design included formal gardens, fountains, and terraces.

**THE VATICAN ♦ PALACE**
Since the sixth century, a papal residence had stood near the old church of St. Peter's. In the fifteenth century, the palace was restored and enlarged. Julius II had Bramante make further modifications in the sixteenth century, including the Belvedere Courtyard addition.

**♦A COLLECTION OF CLASSICAL SCULPTURE**
The first piece to be placed in the Belvedere Courtyard was a Roman statue of Apollo (right), second century AD. Next came the Venus Felix (left), acquired in 1509. In time, as its collection grew, the Belvedere became the world's finest collection of classical sculpture.

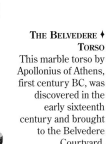

**THE BELVEDERE ♦ TORSO**
This marble torso by Apollonius of Athens, first century BC, was discovered in the early sixteenth century and brought to the Belvedere Courtyard.

**EXCAVATING ♦ THE LAOCOÖN**
In 1506, Julius II appointed Michelangelo superintendent of antiquities. He visited the site where the *Laocoön*, an ancient Greek statue, was found. It made a great impression on him.

**♦ THE LAOCOÖN**
This marble statue was the work of three Greek sculptors in the second and first centuries BC. It was quickly snapped up by Julius II for the Belvedere.

## MICHELANGELO'S LIFE

While he was working on his preliminary drawing for the *Battle of Cascina*, Michelangelo was summoned to Rome by Pope Julius II, who asked him to design his tomb. Julius II was a busy man with a powerful, overbearing personality. Designing his tomb would turn out to be a long and excruciating project for Michelangelo. The artist returned to Florence, where he completed his plan for the Council Chamber and finished another commission. Then, abandoning the *Battle of Cascina* project, he moved to Rome to begin work on the papal tomb. In Rome, he was able to study antiquities firsthand and became known as an expert on classical sculpture. This earned him the position of superintendent of antiquities. In this capacity, he went to see the excavation of the *Laocoön*, an ancient Greek statue discovered among the ruins of a Roman emperor's palace.

# THE DONI TONDO

The *Doni Tondo* is the only finished painting by Michelangelo not done on a wall or a ceiling. It depicts the baby Jesus with his parents, Mary and Joseph. Paintings of the Holy Family were common during the Renaissance. Michelangelo's work includes a group of nude figures in the background. Their meaning is not clear, but may symbolize the classical, or pre-Christian, era. Michelangelo preferred sculpture to painting and the figures in this piece have a three-dimensional, sculptural quality.

**✦ MADDALENA STROZZI**
A portrait by Raphael, 1506 (Galleria Palatina, Florence).

**✦ THE WORK**
*Doni Tondo*, c. 1506, tempera on panel, diameter 47 inches (120 cm), (Uffizi, Florence).
A common theory is that Angelo Doni, a member of one of the leading Florentine families, commissioned the painting to celebrate his marriage to Maddalena Strozzi in January 1504. The Strozzi coat of arms on the frame could support this view. Another theory is that the work was not painted until after the discovery of the *Laocoön* in 1506. The painting shows the influence of ancient Greek culture, and one of the background figures is very similar to the main figure in the *Laocoön*. In this case, the tondo may have been painted to celebrate not a marriage, but the birth of the Doni's first child, Maria, in 1507.

**✦ ANGELO DONI**
A portrait by Raphael, 1506 (Galleria Palatina, Florence).

**✦ THE FRAME**
The carved and gilded wooden frame bears the arms of the Strozzi family: three crescent moons, linked. Surrounding the moons are the heads of four lions.

## A ROUND PAINTING

A *tondo* is a circular work of art. The form had existed in antiquity and was revived during the Renaissance. At that time, round paintings usually were associated with a marriage or a birth. The *Doni Tondo* is still in its original frame, which was designed by Michelangelo. The bright colors in the painting would appear again in his Sistine Chapel frescoes, which he would begin two years later.

**✦ THE LAOCOÖN**
In the *Doni Tondo*, the pose of the nude figure in the background, to the right of Joseph, is similar to that of the middle figure in the *Laocoön*.

♦ **PALMA VECCHIO**
Palma Vecchio was a Venetian artist. His composition of the Holy Family is more traditional than Michelangelo's and includes Mary Magdalene. She holds a vase of ointment, with which she later anointed Christ's feet. The colors and landscape setting are typical of Venetian painting.
*The Holy Family,* 1508–1512 (Uffizi, Florence).

♦ **AGNOLO BRONZINO**
The painting below, by Florentine artist Agnolo Bronzino, was done after Michelangelo's *Doni Tondo* and may have been influenced by it. The colors of the clothing and Joseph's position are similar to Michelangelo's work.
*Holy Family Panciatichi*, 1540 (Uffizi, Florence).

**LUCA SIGNORELLI** ♦
A possible forerunner of Michelangelo's painting is this tondo by Luca Signorelli portraying the same subject. Michelangelo admired this artist, whose painted figures have a sculptural quality similar to his own. 1490–1491 (Uffizi, Florence).

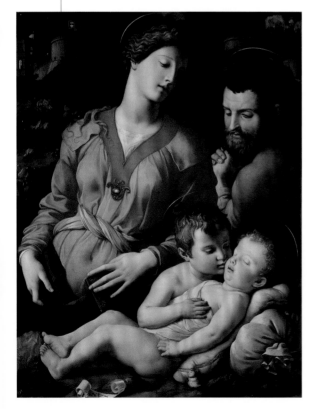

# Papal Rome

In the early sixteenth century, Florence and other centers of Renaissance art were eclipsed by Rome, which was quickly becoming the cultural capital of Europe. This transformation was fueled by the efforts of Pope Julius II, an ambitious ruler and art patron. In addition to his position as head of the Catholic Church, the pope was also a secular ruler of territories in Italy known as the Papal States. In this capacity, popes behaved like other Renaissance rulers: waging war, surrounding themselves with artists and scholars, and commissioning splendid buildings and works of art. The popes used art to symbolize their power and glorify their reigns. Julius II summoned the most talented artists in Italy to his court.

Above: Raphael, *Portrait of Julius II*, 1512 (Uffizi, Florence).

### ♦ Julius II
(1443–1513)
Nephew of Pope Sixtus IV and a member of the della Rovere family, one of the most powerful in Italy, Julius was elected pope in 1503. He began an aggressive campaign to restore papal power throughout the Papal States and expand the Church's influence. He used military and political means to achieve his goals. His readiness to make war earned him the nickname the "Warrior Pope."

Above: Raphael, *Portrait of Leo X with Cardinals Luigi de' Rossi and Giulio de Medici*, detail, 1518 (Uffizi, Florence).

### ♦ Leo X
(1475–1521)
Son of Lorenzo the Magnificent, Leo X was made a cardinal at the age of thirteen and became pope upon the death of Julius II. As a Medici, he often diverted Michelangelo's energies into projects to glorify his family, such as a new facade for the church of San Lorenzo in Florence.

### ♦ Bramante
Soon after arriving in Rome, Donato Bramante was asked to design a building to commemorate the martyrdom of St. Peter. Inspired by ancient temples, he designed this small, circular memorial. Known as the Tempietto, it is emblematic of the High Renaissance.

### ♦ Raphael and Michelangelo
While Michelangelo was working on the Sistine Chapel ceiling, Raphael was decorating the Vatican apartments. In one of his frescoes, *The School of Athens*, Raphael included this portrait of Michelangelo in the guise of the Greek philosopher Heraclitus.

Above: Bronzino, *Portrait of Clement VII*, 1553 (Uffizi, Florence).

✦**CLEMENT VII**
(1478–1534)
Nephew of Lorenzo the Magnificent, he was elected pope in 1523. During his reign, Rome was sacked by troops of Charles V, the Holy Roman Emperor. Clement first opposed Charles, then made an uneasy peace with him that restored the Medici to power in Florence in 1530. Clement VII commissioned Michelangelo to paint the end wall of the Sistine Chapel.

Above: Titian, *Paul III with the Cardinals Alessandro and Ottavio Farnese*, detail, 1546 (Galleria di Capodimonte, Naples).

✦**PAUL III**
(1468–1549)
Following Clement VII as pope in 1534, Paul III led the Catholic Church into the Counter-Reformation. Many of Michelangelo's later works were commissioned by Paul III, including the design and supervision of St. Peter's, the Piazza del Campidoglio, and the Palazzo Farnese in Rome.

✦**RAPHAEL AND THE VATICAN ROOMS**
Julius II invited Raphael to Rome in 1508 to decorate four rooms, called *stanze*, in the Vatican. The rooms were used as private apartments by the pope himself. Raphael completed the frescoes on the walls and ceiling of the Stanza della Segnatura in 1511. The frescoes depict the relationship between Platonic philosophy and Christianity. Raphael, *The School of Athens*, 1508–1511 (Stanza della Segnatura, Vatican Palace, Rome).

✦**MICHELANGELO AND JULIUS II**
This painting by Anastasio Fonte-buoni shows Michelangelo in conversation with Julius II. At such meetings, the pope commissioned new works and received progress reports.

## MICHELANGELO'S LIFE

Working for Pope Julius II was not always easy. He could be unpredictable, changing his mind about what he wanted an artist to do. He was also a busy man, who could keep an artist waiting for hours. When an architect or painter finally had an audience with him, he was often preoccupied with other projects and unable to give his full attention to their concerns. Sometimes he was short of money and couldn't advance the necessary funds to complete a work. Michelangelo experienced all of these situations after the pope hired him to design his tomb. It was a huge project and Michelangelo had already spent eight months in the town of Carrara selecting the marble to be used. The pope, however, was focused on the building of the new church of St. Peter's. Frustrated, Michelangelo left Rome and returned to Florence.

# A Tomb for Julius II

When Julius II first proposed the building of a grand tomb for himself, Michelangelo was excited at the prospect. The design called for no less than forty large statues. The work was commissioned in 1506 and Michelangelo's first task was to go to Carrara to select suitable blocks of marble. He spent months in Carrara and then arranged for the blocks to be moved to Rome. At one point, the Tiber River flooded, submerging the marble. Michelangelo had to wait for the water level to drop before the marble could be retrieved. That was only the beginning of his problems. Over the next forty years, the project would be stalled repeatedly. After the death of Julius in 1513, negotiations with his heirs complicated matters even further until, in 1545, the final, much-reduced monument was erected.

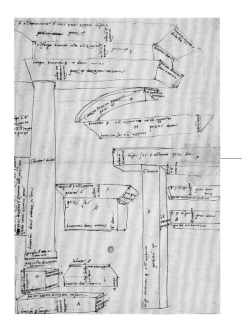

**♦ DETAILED INSTRUCTIONS**
Michelangelo made detailed drawings to explain the number and size of the blocks of marble he would need for a particular project. This drawing from 1521 shows the blocks needed for the facade of the church of San Lorenzo in Florence. Commissions of this kind often interrupted his work on Julius's tomb.

**MICHELANGELO ♦ IN CARRARA**
Michelangelo traveled to the famous marble quarries of Carrara, in Tuscany, to select the marble for Julius's tomb. He even supervised the quarrying, or excavation, of the stone.

**♦ CHANGE OF PLANS**
Michelangelo redesigned the monument many times over the years. His first plan was that it should be free-standing. Later, he decided to place it against a wall. A lack of funds eventually reduced the number of statues originally planned for the tomb. Michelangelo, *Study for the Tomb of Pope Julius II*, (Uffizi, Florence).

**♦ THE FINISHED MONUMENT**
The figure of Moses, bottom center, is the focal point of the composition. It is the only one of the statues that definitely can be attributed to Michelangelo.
*Tomb of Julius II*, 1512–1545 (San Pietro in Vincoli, Rome).

**REBEL SLAVE ♦**
Michelangelo made several statues which were not included in the final monument and for which he never received payment, c. 1513 (Louvre, Paris).

**♦ DYING SLAVE**
Michelangelo, c. 1513 (Louvre, Paris). This statue was meant to stand in one of the niches on the bottom row, along with other similar statues. These figures were clearly inspired by classical sculpture.

**♦ MARBLE**
Marble had been used for statuary since ancient times. While not as strong as bronze, it was often preferred to other materials because it is translucent and can also take a high polish. When selecting a block of marble for carving, an artist had to be sure it was perfectly sound, because small flaws or cracks in the material would cause it to fracture under the sculptor's chisel.

## MICHELANGELO'S LIFE

Despite attempts by Julius II to make him return to Rome, Michelangelo stayed in Florence and resumed work on some of his earlier projects. Julius II finally took action to make the artist return to him. He wrote an official letter to the head of the Florentine Republic, Pier Soderini, who begged Michelangelo not to cause a diplomatic incident by refusing to do what the pope requested. In November 1506, Michelangelo met the pope in Bologna, which the papal army had just captured. He assumed Julius would encourage him to continue his work on the tomb, but instead, the pope ordered him to make a huge bronze statue of himself. In addition, the pope had another new project for Michelangelo: to decorate the ceiling of the Sistine Chapel.

# FRESCO PAINTING

In Italy, artists used a technique called *buon fresco* to paint on walls and ceilings. The word *fresco* means "fresh" in Italian and the technique refers to painting directly on wet, or fresh, plaster. The plaster dries within twelve hours. Because of this, artists had to plan their day carefully, tackling only what could be completed within a twelve-hour period. Once the plaster is dry, it's difficult to go back and make changes. Some artists retouched their work *a secco*, that is, after it had dried. They used tempera, which contained egg yolk. The egg served to bind the paint to the wall. Major changes, however, required removing the plaster completely. In the Sistine Chapel, Michelangelo made small changes *a secco*, but in some cases, had to chip off entire sections of plaster and start over.

**♦ GROTESQUES**
During the Renaissance, small rooms covered in paintings were discovered among the ancient ruins in Rome. They reminded people of grottoes, or caves. Decorating small rooms with whimsical animals, flowers, and other images became fashionable, and the style was known as *grotesque*. Raphael used the style for this bathroom in the Vatican Palace in 1516.

**♦ MICHELANGELO**
Michelangelo used the *a secco* technique to retouch some of his frescoes in the Sistine Chapel. The technique is clearly visible in the hair of the figure on the left.

**♦ GIULIO ROMANO**
Giulio Romano was a pupil of Raphael and a brilliant fresco painter. In a room of the Palazzo Te in Mantua, he created spectacular mythological scenes, such as this *Aristocratic Banquet,* c. 1526.

## MICHELANGELO'S LIFE

Michelangelo finished the bronze statue of Julius II in 1507. In May 1508, he signed the contract with the pope to paint the Sistine Chapel ceiling. It was an enormous undertaking, and Michelangelo had little experience with frescoes. He was apprehensive, yet he embraced the responsibility and even enlarged on the pope's original plan. For four years, from May 1508 until October 1512, he worked on the ceiling without a break. He built a platform 66 feet (20 meters) high. He stood on the platform to paint, but it was a great physical strain. He sent to Florence for paints and assistants, but soon decided to tackle the work all on his own.

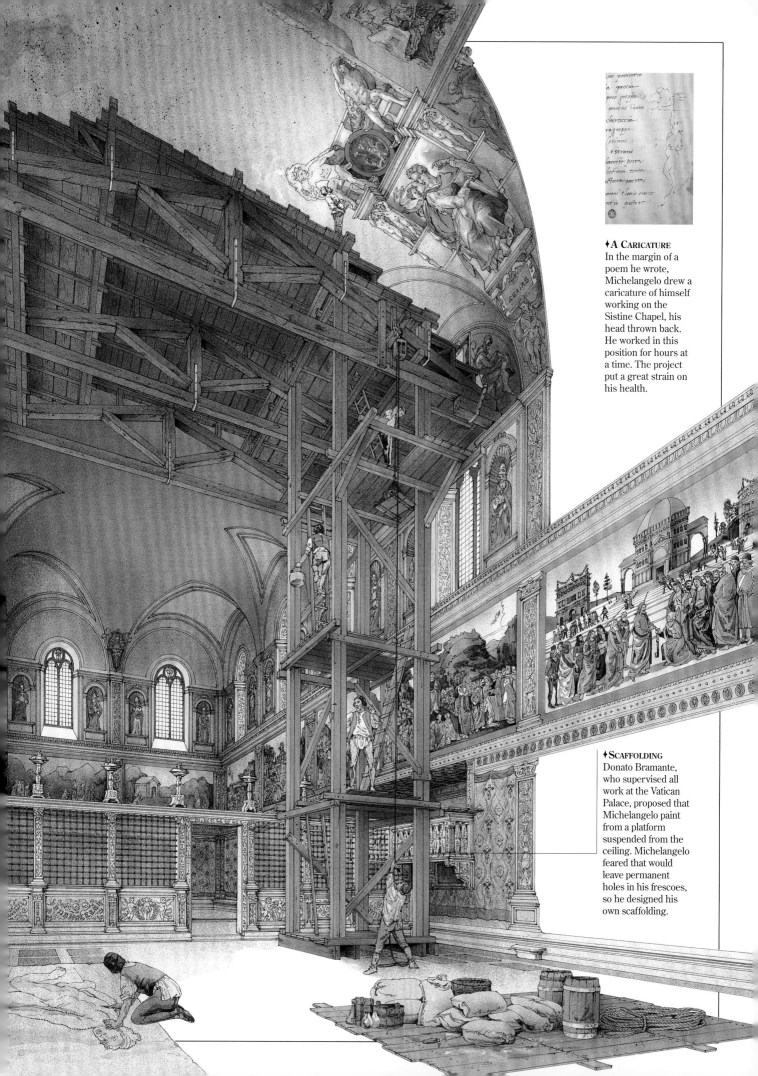

### ♦ A CARICATURE
In the margin of a poem he wrote, Michelangelo drew a caricature of himself working on the Sistine Chapel, his head thrown back. He worked in this position for hours at a time. The project put a great strain on his health.

### ♦ SCAFFOLDING
Donato Bramante, who supervised all work at the Vatican Palace, proposed that Michelangelo paint from a platform suspended from the ceiling. Michelangelo feared that would leave permanent holes in his frescoes, so he designed his own scaffolding.

# SUBJECTS FOR THE SISTINE CEILING

Julius II approached Michelangelo with a plan to paint the twelve apostles on the Sistine Chapel ceiling. Michelangelo had something more complicated in mind. His final frescoes contain over 300 figures. The walls of the chapel featured scenes from the Bible's New Testament. Michelangelo chose subjects from the Old Testament for his ceiling. The rectangular panels in the center depict episodes from the book of Genesis. They are surrounded by prophets and other biblical figures.

♦ **GOD AS CREATOR**
The first five panels in the middle of the ceiling show scenes from the Creation. In the third panel, above, God is shown separating the land from the sea and creating birds and fish. The latter were painted *a secco,* which fades over time, and are no longer visible.

♦ **THE WORK**
*Ceiling of the Sistine Chapel*, 1508–1512, fresco on masonry, 44 x 134 feet (13 x 40 m) (Sistine Chapel, Vatican Palace, Rome).
The Sistine Chapel, named after Pope Sixtus IV, was one of the most important rooms in the Vatican and the place where new popes were elected. The walls had already been painted during the fifteenth century and the ceiling was decorated to look like a starry sky, with gold stars on a blue background. The ceiling had been damaged, however, and Julius II, nephew of Pope Sixtus IV, hired Michelangelo to repaint it. Julius's plan was to paint the twelve apostles in the triangular sections of the ceiling and a geometrical pattern on the vault. Michelangelo had more ambitious plans, which the pope agreed to. With the scaffolding in place, he set to work in July 1508. He had a few assistants at the start, but was unhappy with their work and completed the ceiling single-handedly between August 1508 and October 1512.

♦ **DETAIL**
One of the bronze medallions that Michelangelo paint-ed on the ceiling.

## Painting the Ceiling
Michelangelo painted the nine scenes in the center of the ceiling first. The frescoes on the left, which contain many small figures, are the earliest. His later scenes featured fewer and larger figures. He chose bright colors for his frescoes so they would be more visible from the floor of the chapel.

♦ **A MULTITUDE OF IMAGES**
The frescoes on the Sistine Chapel ceiling cover over 10,000 square feet (1,000 square meters) and include some 300 figures. To bring order to the multitude of figures represented, Michelangelo divided the ceiling into sections, including nine rectangular panels in the center, eight triangular sections along the sides, and numerous painted niches.

### ♦ ADAM AND EVE

The sixth panel presents two related episodes: Original Sin and the Expulsion of Adam and Eve from the Garden of Eden. A tree with a serpent coiled around its trunk separates the two scenes. The tree represents good and evil. The Archangel Gabriel is at the top of the tree.

### ♦ CHRIST'S ANCESTORS

The base of the vault is lined with a series of triangular and semi-circular areas. In these sections, Michelangelo painted the ancestors of Christ, as mentioned in the Gospel of St. Matthew. Above is a detail from one of the semi-circular areas, known as a lunette.

### ♦ THE PROPHET JEREMIAH

Seven prophets from the Bible appear seated in niches along both sides of the ceiling. Here, Jeremiah, who prophesied that the people of Judah would be punished for disobeying God, is sitting in sorrowful thought.

### ♦ THE CREATION OF ADAM

Perhaps the most famous image on the chapel ceiling is Michelangelo's portrayal of God giving life to Adam. Their two hands form the focal point of the scene.

### ♦ THE SIBYLS

Sibyls were female prophets in antiquity. They are not mentioned in the Bible. Legends invented in the Middle Ages, however, made it seem that the sibyls had foreseen the coming of Jesus. Michelangelo therefore portrayed the sibyls alongside the biblical prophets. There are five sibyls on the ceiling. The Persian Sibyl, above, was said to have foretold the triumphs of Alexander the Great.

# The Structure of the Sistine Ceiling

To create a unifying structure for the ceiling, Michelangelo enclosed his figures in a grid of imaginary architecture. A painted cornice frames the nine central scenes. Below the cornice are a series of painted pillars that follow the curve of the vault. Between the pillars are niches where the prophets sit on marble blocks. The triangular sections, called spandrels, were real architectural features, but Michelangelo painted them to look like frescoes. The architectural grid helped to separate scenes and bring order to the composition.

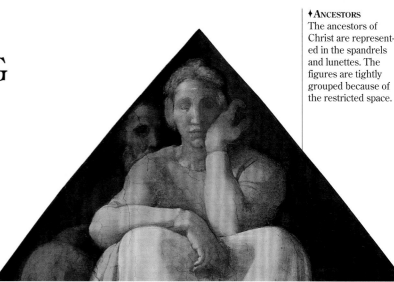

**✦Ancestors**
The ancestors of Christ are represented in the spandrels and lunettes. The figures are tightly grouped because of the restricted space.

### The Proper Perspective
The Sistine Chapel ceiling was both curved and 68 feet (20.7 m) above the floor. This presented special challenges for Michelangelo. To make his figures look "correct" from that height and on a curved surface, he had to disregard the rules of perspective used by early Renaissance painters. He used foreshortening and altered the proportions of his figures to achieve the desired effect.

**✦Sibyls and Prophets**
In the tall, rectangular niches along the sides of the ceiling, five sibyls alternate with seven biblical prophets. The prophets are seated on what appear to be marble thrones projecting from the vault. The role of these niches in the overall composition is to visually anchor the panels in the center of the ceiling and connect them to the spandrels, or triangular sections, along the edges.
Above left: the Libyan Sibyl; and right: the Prophet Jeremiah.

**✦ BRONZE FIGURES**
The figures arranged in mirror-image pairs above the spandrels are painted to resemble bronze statues. Between them is an ox skull, a common motif in classical decoration. To paint these figures, Michelangelo used a cartoon. A cartoon, common in fresco painting, was a full-size drawing done on paper and then "traced" onto a wall or ceiling. For these pairs, the cartoon for one figure was merely reversed to obtain its twin.

**✦ PUTTI**
Often naked and winged, putti were representations of small children in Renaissance art.

**✦ NUDE FIGURES**
The panels in the center of the ceiling are surrounded by groups of male nudes. The figures help to frame each individual scene. Their superbly rendered physiques are reminiscent of classical sculpture. It's possible they were meant to represent the beauty of humankind created in the image of God. The figures were probably based on life drawings, which Michelangelo then idealized and repeated in a number of variations.

**HOMAGE TO ✦ THE POPES**
Garlands and cornucopias filled with oak leaves and acorns are an allusion to the della Rovere family, to which Popes Sixtus IV and his nephew Julius II belonged. In Italian, *rovere* is a species of oak.

# SAN LORENZO

The church of San Lorenzo was one of the oldest in Florence. It was also the parish church of the powerful Medici family. The church was substantially rebuilt during the Renaissance. The most talented Florentine artists were involved in its reconstruction. Filippo Brunelleschi, who had designed the great dome of the Florence Cathedral, Donatello, and Verrocchio each made contributions during the fifteenth century. In the sixteenth century, Pope Leo X, a Medici, asked Michelangelo to design a new facade for the church. Although that project was never completed, Michelangelo designed the New Sacristy (a small chapel), the Laurentian Library (a private Medici library), and two Medici tombs.

**✦ THE CUPOLA**
The imposing dome crowning the Princes' Chapel was erected in the seventeenth century. A monument to Medici vanity, it dwarfs the domes of the two earlier chapels.

**✦ THE PRINCES' CHAPEL**
This chapel, added in the seventeenth century, was built entirely of marble and semi-precious stones. It holds Medici tombs.

**✦ THE OLD SACRISTY**
The first chapel intended to house the Medici tombs was built by Filippo Brunelleschi between 1421 and 1428. He used a straightforward geometrical style with very simple decoration.

**✦ THE ENTRANCE TO THE LIBRARY**
The library's entrance is dominated by the dramatic stairway designed by Michelangelo.

**THE LIBRARY ✦**
Michelangelo designed the Laurentian Library. It was started as a private library by Cosimo the Elder, father of Lorenzo the Magnificent, and contains precious fifteenth-century manuscripts. In the Renaissance, libraries were often located in convents.

## MICHELANGELO'S LIFE

While Michelangelo was in Rome working on the Sistine Chapel, Florence lost its republican freedoms and was once again under Medici rule. Giuliano of Nemours, son of Lorenzo the Magnificent, ruled the city. In 1513, his brother Giovanni succeeded Julius II as Pope Leo X. The political connection between Rome and Florence left Michelangelo little choice: he was bound to be employed by members of the Medici family. In Rome, he lived in a modest house in the Via Macel de' Corvi, where he maintained a simple lifestyle. He continued working on Julius II's tomb, but was soon interrupted by the new Medici pope, who asked Michelangelo to design a facade for the remodeled church of San Lorenzo.

**♦ THE NEW SACRISTY**
Michelangelo made the new chapel exactly the same size as Brunelleschi's Old Sacristy. He did not decorate the walls, but relied on a combination of sculpture and architecture to create an austere but powerful design.

**A MODEL ♦**
In 1516, Michelangelo signed a contract to design the facade for San Lorenzo. He worked on it for two years, making several studies and this wooden model, but had to abandon the project to concentrate on the New Sacristy. (Casa Buonarroti, Florence).

**♦ THE FACADE**
Although Michelangelo drew up plans for the facade of San Lorenzo, work proceeded slowly and appears to have stopped when Pope Leo X died in 1521. The facade was never finished.

# THE MEDICI TOMBS

In his tombs for two Medici dukes, Lorenzo of Urbino and Giuliano of Nemours, Michelangelo departed from the traditional practice of decorating tombs with Christian symbols, such as angels or the Virgin Mary. Instead, he used allegorical figures — Day and Night and Dawn and Dusk — to represent the passage of time. His Medici tombs are much simpler than his design for Julius II's tomb. Stripped of excess decoration and statuary, each features a sarcophagus, or stone coffin, at the base and three figures, including a statue of the duke at the top, set against an architectural background.

Above and below: details of the two tombs.

✦**THE WORK**
*Tombs of Dukes Lorenzo of Urbino and Giuliano of Nemours,* 1524–1534, marble (New Sacristy, San Lorenzo, Florence). In 1520, Pope Leo X and his cousin, Giulio de Medici, who later became Pope Clement VII, commissioned Michelangelo to design funeral monuments for four of their Medici relatives: Lorenzo the Magnificent; his brother Giuliano; Lorenzo's son, Giuliano, the Duke of Nemours; and Lorenzo's grandson, Lorenzo, the Duke of Urbino. Michelangelo drew up a number of plans for the monument. His initial idea was to construct a square, free-standing tomb in the center of the chapel, but he later chose a combination of architecture and sculpture set against the walls. He went to Carrara in 1521 to select the marble, but progress was slow after that. Work came to a halt in 1534 when he settled permanently in Rome. In the end, he finished only two of the tombs — those of the two young dukes.

✦**THE TWO DUKES**
The figures of Lorenzo (above) and Giuliano (below) are idealized portraits, expressing their inner nature more than their physical attributes. Lorenzo is shown in a pensive attitude. Giuliano appears confident.

**A MARRIAGE OF ARCHITECTURE AND SCULPTURE**
Michelangelo's monuments to the two dukes are both powerful and serene and a perfect blend of architecture and sculpture. The architectural elements, including columns, niches, windows, and garlands, show the influence of classical art. The face of the figure of Giuliano is also similar to ancient Greek statuary and Michelangelo's *David*.

**♦ DAWN AND DUSK**
Left and right: the figures of Dawn and Dusk from the Tomb of Lorenzo.
The periods of light just before sunrise and just after sunset are brief. On the tomb of Lorenzo, the figures of Dawn and Dusk are poignant reminders of the passage of time and the fleeting quality of human life.

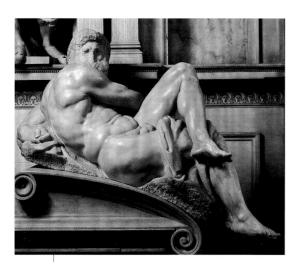

**♦ DAY AND NIGHT**
Above: The figures of Day and Night from the tomb of Giuliano. The figure of Day (top) is alert, with limbs full of tension, reflecting the preoccupations of daytime. Night (bottom), on the other hand, is a figure in repose. She wears a crown with a star and crescent moon, and her foot rests on a cushion decorated with poppies — a symbol of sleep. The owl behind her foot is a creature of the night.

**♦ RISING FROM THE TOMB**
On both tombs, the opposing nature of the allegorical figures is emphasized by their position — with their backs to each other. Between the figures, there appears to be an opening in the lid of the sarcophagus. It is almost as if the weight and twisting forms of the figures have opened the lid and created a space for the soul to escape. The statue of the duke, immediately above, may represent the soul's ascension to a higher level of existence beyond death.

# FORTIFICATIONS

The Renaissance is known as a period of artistic achievement, but it was also an era of almost constant warfare, particularly on the Italian peninsula. In 1527, the troops of Charles V, Holy Roman Emperor, had sacked Rome. In 1529, they threatened Florence. The city, hoping to avoid Rome's fate, prepared for an attack. It placed Michelangelo in charge of fortifications and asked him, as an architect, to modernize the city's defenses. The arrival of cannons in the fourteenth century had revolutionized warfare in Europe. Tall castle walls were no longer an effective defense. Michelangelo designed bastions with low, irregular walls that were more resistant to cannonfire and provided space for the defenders' own cannons.

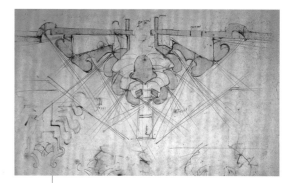

**♦ MICHELANGELO'S DESIGNS**
Michelangelo's many drawings of bastions show his ability to combine artistic shapes with practical considerations. Instead of the traditional square structures, which were unequal to the challenge of the new offensive strategies, he designed more organic shapes. This drawing from 1528 shows one such structure. The curved sections protruding from the bastion are reminiscent of the claws of a crab. (Casa Buonarroti, Florence).

**MICHELANGELO'S LIFE**
After working for two years on the facade of San Lorenzo, Michelangelo was interrupted again by Pope Leo X, who now asked him to design tombs for the Medici family inside the church. Michelangelo diverted his energies to this new commission. At San Lorenzo, Michelangelo was able to use his talents as both architect and sculptor. In 1521, Pope Leo X died and was succeeded in turn by Adrian VI and Clement VII, who was a Medici. Clement VII witnessed the sacking of Rome. The Florentines took advantage of the subsequent chaos to revolt against the Medici and restore republican rule once more. Soon, however, Florence itself was facing an impending assault and the republic hired Michelangelo to design fortifications. He stopped work on all other projects to concentrate on the city's defense.

The siege of
Florence lasted ten
months, ending in
August 1530, when
Charles V's troops
entered the city and
the Medici returned
to power. Giorgio
Vasari painted this
fresco of the siege in
1555–1562 (Palazzo
Vecchio, Florence).

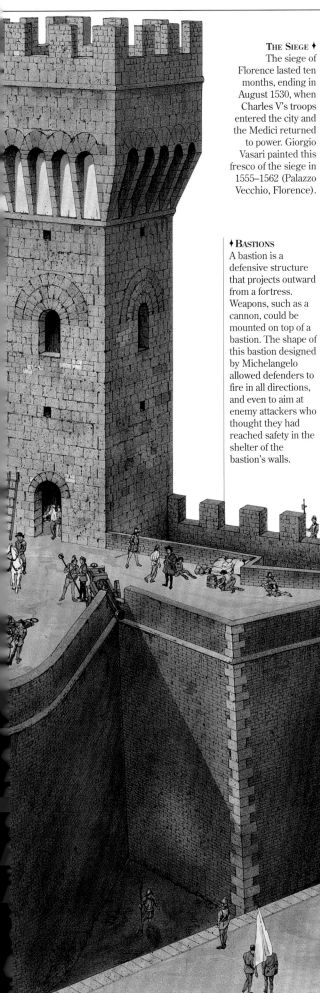

**✦ BASTIONS**
A bastion is a
defensive structure
that projects outward
from a fortress.
Weapons, such as a
cannon, could be
mounted on top of a
bastion. The shape of
this bastion designed
by Michelangelo
allowed defenders to
fire in all directions,
and even to aim at
enemy attackers who
thought they had
reached safety in the
shelter of the
bastion's walls.

**✦ CHARLES V**
Titian, *Emperor
Charles V on
Horseback,* detail,
1548 (Prado, Madrid).

**✦ MICHELANGELO**
Matteo Rosselli,
*Michelangelo as
Commissioner for
Fortifications,*
1615–1637 (Casa
Buonarroti,
Florence).

# RETURN OF THE MEDICI

Following the sack of Rome, Pope Clement VII formed an alliance with Charles V, who agreed to restore Medici rule to Florence. His troops besieged the city for ten months between 1529 and 1530. The city's eventual defeat marked the end of the Republic of Florence and the return of the Medici, who would remain in power until the eighteenth century. The most notorious Medici ruler of the sixteenth century was Cosimo I. He was a shrewd and ambitious ruler who laid siege to cities, including Siena, until his power extended over all of Tuscany. At the same time, he promoted the arts as a way of enhancing the prestige of Florence and the Medici dynasty.

**♦ Cosimo I**
This bust by Benvenuto Cellini, 1545 (Museo del Bargello, Florence) portrays Cosimo I (1519–1574) as a Roman emperor. His autocratic style resembled that of an emperor. Having become duke in 1537, Cosimo improved his position further by marrying Eleanora of Toledo, daughter of the powerful Spanish viceroy in Italy. In 1569, the pope elevated him to the rank of grand duke, higher than any other Italian prince.

**♦ The Port of Livorno**
Cosimo I built the Florentine navy and expanded the port of Livorno.

**Siena ♦**
Giorgio Vasari made a wooden model of Siena for Cosimo I. It was useful in helping the duke decide how to besiege the city, which he eventually conquered.

**♦ Models**
During the Renaissance, it was common practice for architects to make models of their building projects, in order to show their patrons how they intended to carry out their plans.

**A Palace ♦ at Arezzo**
A model of a residence in Arezzo designed by Giorgio Vasari.

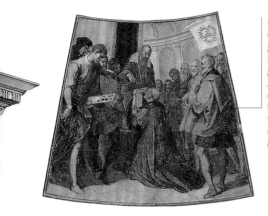

### ♦ COSIMO I'S ACADEMY

Cosimo I was a fierce ruler, but he was also a great patron of the arts. He was responsible for some of the most famous buildings and gardens in Florence and founded the Accademia dell'Arte del Disegno (Academy of Art and Design). The event is celebrated in this fresco. Today, the art gallery that adjoins the school, called the Accademia, contains some of the greatest masterpieces of Italian art, including Michelangelo's *David*.

### GIORGIO VASARI ♦
(1511–1574)

Vasari was a painter and architect who enjoyed Medici patronage. One of his most famous works is the Uffizi Palace, designed as administrative headquarters for Cosimo I. It is now one of the world's oldest art galleries.

### ♦ THE UFFIZI
Vasari had a wooden model made of his project for the Uffizi Palace.

## MICHELANGELO'S LIFE

Despite the fierce resistance of many of its citizens, including Michelangelo, Florence eventually fell to the troops under Charles V in August 1530. This signaled the permanent loss of its republican freedoms and the return of Medici rule. Although he had supported the republicans, Michelangelo received a pardon from Clement VII and returned to his work on the Medici tombs at San Lorenzo. In 1531, Michelangelo lost both his father and a brother. He himself was nearly sixty, and in letters he wrote at the time, he expressed his own fears about death. Clement VII called Michelangelo to Rome in 1533 and asked him to paint the vast fresco of *The Last Judgment* on the end wall of the Sistine Chapel. Michelangelo returned to Florence briefly, and in 1534, he left his native city, never to return.

# THEATER AND LITERATURE

High culture during the sixteenth century centered on the courts and palaces of the ruling families. They supported not only the visual arts, but theater and literature as well. In Florence, the Medici provided spectacular entertainment for special occasions. They also staged an annual season of theatrical events and hired some of the leading artists of the day to design scenery and costumes. In literature, poetry enjoyed great popularity. Michelangelo wrote close to 300 poems. His poetry was private, however, and not meant for publication. His poems explored serious themes, such as religion and the nature of love. He shared them only with a few intimate friends, including the poet Vittoria Colonna, whom he met in Rome.

**✦ VITTORIA COLONNA**
Michelangelo met the noblewoman and poet Vittoria Colonna in Rome in 1536. She became one of his closest friends, sharing his enthusiasm for religion, art, and poetry. This portrait of her is attributed to Sebastiano del Piombo. *Portrait of Vittoria Colonna*, c. 1535 (Museo di Palazzo Venezia, Rome).

**✦ BUONTALENTI**
One of the first permanent theaters was constructed in the Uffizi Palace around 1585. It was designed by Bernardo Buontalenti. An architect, painter, and engineer, Buontalenti also designed scenery for the stage. This drawing shows one of his set designs (Uffizi, Florence).

**✦ COSTUMES**
Like many artists of his time, Buontalenti also designed costumes for the theater. This drawing from 1589 shows some of his designs (National Library, Florence).

**✦ MICHELANGELO'S LONELINESS**
Though patronized by wealthy rulers, Michelangelo distanced himself from court life. His letters tell of his loneliness as an artist. On February 22, 1556, he wrote to Vasari, "It has pleased God . . . to let me live on in this fickle world with so many troubles . . . and I can look forward to nothing but endless misery." Above: Giorgio Vasari, *Cosimo I and the Artists of his Court*, 1555–1562 (Palazzo Vecchio, Florence).

**♦A NAVAL BATTLE**
As part of the wedding celebrations for Ferdinando de Medici and Christine of Lorraine in May 1589, the Medici staged an extravagant mock naval battle in the Pitti Palace.

**♦SHIPS**
The courtyard of the palace was lined with waterproof materials and then flooded. It could accommodate up to eighteen ships of various shapes and sizes.

Above and below: details from *The Last Judgment.*

♦ **THE WORK**
*The Last Judgment,* fresco, 1536–1541, 45 x 40 feet (13.7 x 12.2 m) (Sistine Chapel, Rome). Michelangelo was still working on the Medici tombs when Clement VII announced his wish that the artist paint the end wall of the Sistine Chapel. Michelangelo went to Rome to sign the contract and moved there permanently in May 1534. Clement died before work began on the project, but the new pope, Paul III, confirmed the commission. The scaffolding was erected in the spring of 1535 and Michelangelo began work the following year. The massive painting spans the entire wall and took Michelangelo six years to complete. His new fresco was unveiled on October 31, 1541. Within weeks, it was being harshly criticized by defenders of public morality, who found the nude figures in the work indecent. Such criticism continued for years until, in 1564, the figures were painted over with loincloths.

# THE LAST JUDGMENT

Twenty years after finishing the Sistine Chapel ceiling, Michelangelo was called back by Pope Clement VII, who asked him to paint the end wall of the chapel. The subject of the enormous fresco is The Last Judgment. In the Bible, the Gospel according to Saint Matthew warns of a time when Christ will return to Earth to separate the good from the bad and send them to heaven or hell. It was a theme of central importance to Christian believers and a subject that had been depicted by European artists since the Middle Ages.

## PREPARATION

Michelangelo did a great deal of preparatory work for his new undertaking. He did numerous drawings and even modified the surface of the chapel wall so that it sloped slightly outward at the top. This prevented dust from settling on the fresco and also improved the perspective. The sculptural figures in the work are reminiscent of those on the Medici tombs, which he had just completed.

♦ **MOSAIC**
This mosaic, c. 1225, is an earlier example of an artwork depicting The Last Judgment. As usual in such scenes, Christ sits in the center as judge. The mosaic decorates the cupola of the Florence Baptistry.

♦ **ST. BARTHOLOMEW**
St. Bartholomew, who was flayed alive, is one of the martyrs portrayed in Michelangelo's fresco. With biting humor, the artist painted his own face on the skin the saint is holding.

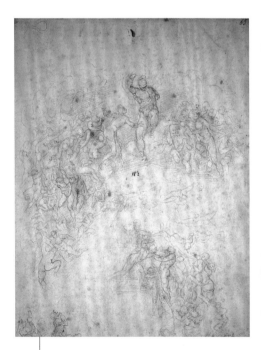

♦ **A STUDY**
In this preliminary drawing, Michelangelo was working out a way to give the figure of Christ enough dynamism to make him the focal point of the whole composition.

♦**SYMBOLS OF CHRIST**
Symbols of Christ's passion are at the top of the fresco. Angels carry the cross and the crown of thorns.

♦**THE COMPOSITION**
Conceived as a single scene, the fresco has a clear arrangement. Christ the judge occupies the center and is flanked by the Virgin Mary. Near him are saints and the saved. The bottom, darker portion of the painting represents hell.

♦**THE SAVED**
The saved are shown floating up toward heaven. Some of the saved reach down to help lift the others.

**ANGELS** ♦
In the center of the lower part of the fresco, angels blow their trumpets, summoning all humankind to judgment. They hold two books: the smaller book holds the names of the saved.

**CHARON** ♦
Charon, the ferryman of the dead, discharges damned souls from his boat.

♦**MARTYRS**
Christian martyrs are represented in the middle section of the fresco. They bear the symbols of their martyrdom. St. Catherine, for example, is shown holding a wheel.

53

# MICHELANGELO IN ROME

In their quest to restore Rome to its former glory, Renaissance popes commissioned new building projects throughout the city. Despite the destruction caused by Charles V's troops in 1527, Rome continued to expand, and architects flocked to the papal court. Michelangelo settled permanently in Rome in 1534, and during the next thirty years — the final years of his life — he created some of his greatest masterpieces. Though he had come to Rome to paint the end wall of the Sistine Chapel, much of his work during this period consisted of architectural projects. He designed a new city gate, the Porta Pia, converted ancient Roman baths into the church of Santa Maria degli Angeli, and became chief architect of St. Peter's. In 1536, he began redesigning the Piazza del Campidoglio. The piazza was the center of Rome's civic government, and Michelangelo's transformation of the space is considered one of his major achievements.

**♦ THE PIAZZA UNDER CONSTRUCTION**
This etching, c. 1547, shows the Piazza del Campidoglio in the early stages of construction. Michelangelo died before the work was complete, but the final plaza remains faithful to his original design.

**♦ SANTA MARIA DEGLI ANGELI**
In 1561, Pope Pius IV approved Michelangelo's plans to transform a group of large, ancient Roman baths into the church of Santa Maria degli Angeli. The church was built within the remaining ruins of the baths. Pius IV is buried in the church.

## MICHELANGELO'S LIFE
Pope Clement VII died shortly before Michelangelo arrived in Rome in September 1534, but his successor, Pope Paul III, admired Michelangelo's work and confirmed the commission of *The Last Judgment*. Michelangelo returned to his house in the Via Macel de' Corvi. During this period, he met the poet Vittoria Colonna, with whom he formed a close and long-lasting friendship. They exchanged letters, poems, and ideas about religion. Michelangelo began painting *The Last Judgment* while continuing to work on the tomb for Julius II. Though he was in his sixties, he had the energy to take on additional projects, including the demanding architectural commissions of the Piazza del Campidoglio and St. Peter's.

**♦ THE PORTA PIA**
In 1561, Pope Pius IV asked Michelangelo to design a *porta*, or doorway, in the city walls at the end of the Via Pia. The Via Pia was a new street, named after the pope and laid out on his orders. Michelangelo designed an arched gateway, but construction wasn't finished until after his death. The top of the final gate differs from his original plan.

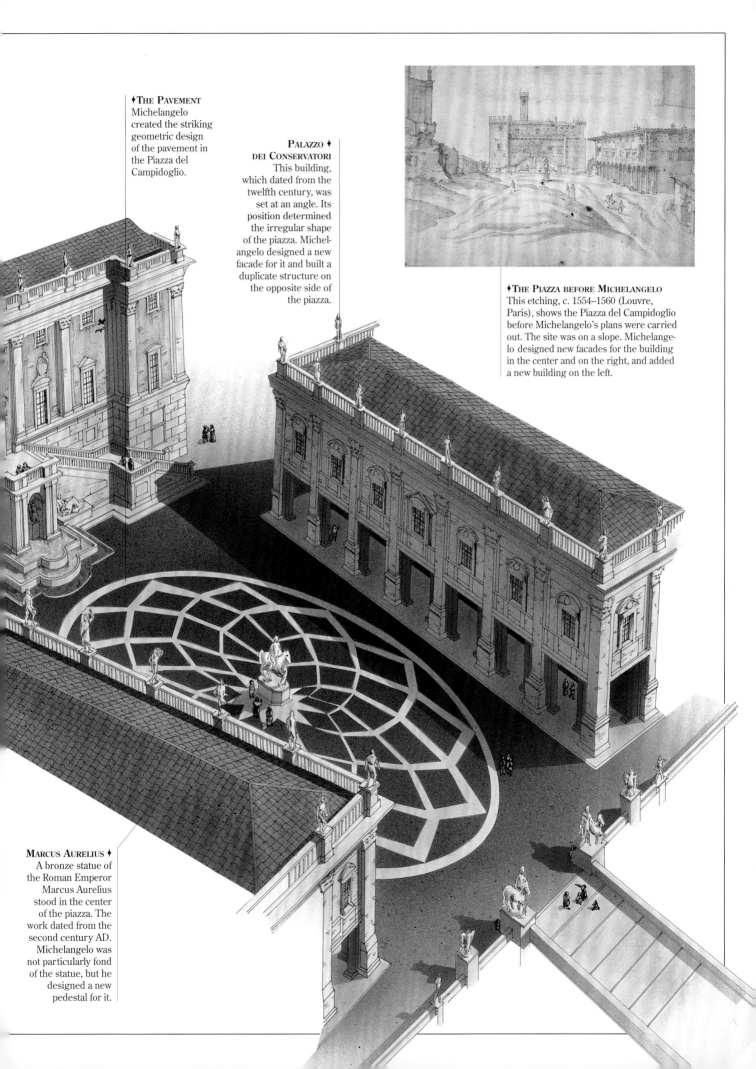

**♦ THE PAVEMENT**
Michelangelo created the striking geometric design of the pavement in the Piazza del Campidoglio.

**PALAZZO ♦ DEI CONSERVATORI**
This building, which dated from the twelfth century, was set at an angle. Its position determined the irregular shape of the piazza. Michelangelo designed a new facade for it and built a duplicate structure on the opposite side of the piazza.

**♦ THE PIAZZA BEFORE MICHELANGELO**
This etching, c. 1554–1560 (Louvre, Paris), shows the Piazza del Campidoglio before Michelangelo's plans were carried out. The site was on a slope. Michelangelo designed new facades for the building in the center and on the right, and added a new building on the left.

**MARCUS AURELIUS ♦**
A bronze statue of the Roman Emperor Marcus Aurelius stood in the center of the piazza. The work dated from the second century AD. Michelangelo was not particularly fond of the statue, but he designed a new pedestal for it.

# ST. PETER'S

Almost all of the great Renaissance architects who were active in Rome had a hand in the rebuilding of St. Peter's. When Michelangelo took over the project in 1547, he considered the plans of his predecessors and rejected most of them, while retaining the ideas of Bramante, the original architect on the project. He was highly critical of Antonio da Sangallo, the architect who immediately preceded him. This caused problems for Michelangelo because many of the workers still on the project were loyal to Sangallo. The pope also put pressure on the artist, asking for frequent progress reports. As chief architect, Michelangelo supervised construction and redesigned parts of the church's interior, but his greatest concern was the dome that would crown the great edifice. In designing it, he took inspiration from Brunelleschi's dome for the Florence Cathedral.

Above: a window and pairs of columns on the dome's drum.

♦ **MICHELANGELO AND ST. PETER'S**
After Bramante, Raphael, Antonio da Sangallo the Younger, and Baldassarre Peruzzi, it fell to Michelangelo to direct the building of St. Peter's and organize the huge construction site that had grown up around the church. Pope Paul III appointed him chief architect in January 1547. At seventy-one, Michelangelo was a bit reluctant to take on such an enormous task. The pope, however, gave him free reign in all matters. He also offered him a large sum of money, but Michelangelo viewed the job as a labor of love and his duty to God. For the last eighteen years of his life, he devoted most of his energy to the project. He modified the design of the church's interior as well as its exterior, and designed its crowning dome. The dome was not finished until after Michelangelo's death and is more vertical than the rounded dome he had designed.

♦ **A MODEL OF THE DOME**
To demonstrate his plans for the dome, Michelangelo made a huge wooden model of a section of the dome, showing both its interior and exterior. The model can still be seen in the Vatican today.

♦ **THE FINISHED CHURCH**
Louis Haghe, *The Church of St. Peter's, Rome, seen from the Square,* 1868 (Victoria and Albert Museum, London).

♦ **PRESENTING THE MODEL**
Using a large wooden model, Michelangelo explains his plans for the dome to the pope and his cardinals.

## ✦ THE LANTERN
The lantern, or top, of the dome, is very ornate. It was designed by Giacomo della Porta and built by Domenico Fontana, the same team that finished the church's dome.

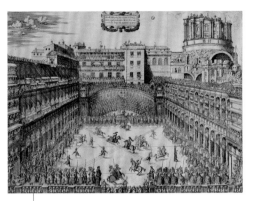

## ✦ JOUSTING IN THE VATICAN
This print by Jacob Binck, c. 1565, shows the Belvedere Courtyard being used for a jousting tournament. St. Peter's can be seen in the background, on the right. Construction of the dome is in progress, with the drum, or base, of the dome almost finished.

## ✦ INSPIRED BY BRUNELLESCHI
Michelangelo took the idea of vertical ribs from Brunelleschi's dome for the Florence Cathedral.

## ✦ THE INTERNAL DOME
Like the dome of the Florence Cathedral, the dome of St. Peter's is a double dome. This part of the model shows Michelangelo's plan for the interior of the dome.

## ✦ BRUNELLESCHI'S DOME
Michelangelo took the idea of building a double vault, with an internal dome enclosed in an outer shell, from Brunelleschi's design for the Florence Cathedral dome (above). In Brunelleschi's dome, which was built between 1420 and 1436, the influence of Gothic architecture is visible: the segments, or sections, between the ribs, are rather angular and the white ribs stand out sharply against the red terracotta tiles. Simplicity and geometrical rigor characterize this early Renaissance masterpiece.

## ✦ MICHELANGELO'S DOME
The structure of Michelangelo's dome is hard to discern beneath its wealth of decorative features. The drum, or base, of the dome is concealed by a ring of windows separated by pairs of columns. The segments of the dome are embellished with small openings on three levels. The lantern is more elaborate than that of the Florentine dome. As in his Medici tombs, Michelangelo's dome is a merging of architecture and sculpture.

# PIETÀS

A pietà is a work of art that depicts the Virgin Mary supporting the dead body of Christ after he has been taken down from the cross. Sometimes additional figures, such as Mary Magdalene, are included. During the Renaissance, pietàs were common in both sculpture and painting. Michelangelo produced four pietàs. The first, created when he was only twenty-four years old, is located in St. Peter's and is probably the most famous pietà in the world.

**✦THE FACE OF CHRIST**
A detail from the *Florence Pietà,* 1550–1555.

**✦THE WORK**
Michelangelo, *Florence Pietà,* c. 1550–1555, marble, 89 inches (226 cm) high (Museo dell'Opera del Duomo, Florence). According to his biographers, Michelangelo intended this sculpture for his own tomb. He sold it, however, in 1561 and it ultimately came into the hands of Tiberio Calcagni, a sculptor and pupil of Michelangelo, who made some major changes to the work. The sculpture was transported to Florence in 1674, on the orders of Grand Duke Cosimo III, and set up in San Lorenzo, the Medici family church. In 1721, it was moved to the Florence Cathedral, where it stood behind the high altar. It is now in a museum.

**✦IN THE CATHEDRAL**
A nineteenth-century print shows the position of the pietà in the Florence Cathedral.

**RONDANINI PIETÀ ✦**
Michelangelo's last pietà was never finished. 1552–1564 (Castello Sforzesco, Milano).

**A STUDY ✦**
Michelangelo made this drawing representing the figure of the dead Christ (Louvre, Paris). It demonstrates both his drawing skill and his understanding of human anatomy.

## FLORENCE PIETÀ

This pietà's most striking feature is the sliding, twisting body of Christ. The face of the bearded figure behind him is thought to be Michelangelo's. While working on this pietà, Michelangelo became so dissatisfied that he attacked it, breaking off piece including Christ's left leg. The unfinished work late became the property of sculptor Tiberio Calcagni, who finished the figure of Mary Magdalene. Her body is too small compared to the other figures and her face is not in the syle of Michelangelo.

**♦ VATICAN PIETÀ**
This is the first and most well-known of Michelangelo's four pietàs. In this version, the Virgin Mary supports the limp body of Christ across her knees. 1498–1499 (St. Peter's, Rome).

**GIOTTO ♦**
Mary's grief after the death of Christ was a common theme of European art in the fourteenth century. Giotto used the subject for one of his frescoes in the Scrovegni Chapel in Padua. His work displayed a realism and emotional quality rare for the time. Giotto, *The Lamentation,* 1302–1306.

**GIOVANNI BELLINI ♦**
A pietà by Venetian painter Giovanni Bellini. *Dead Christ Supported by the Madonna and St. John,* 1460 (Brera, Milan).

**♦ PALESTRINA PIETÀ**
This pietà was one of Michelangelo's last works. The dramatic tension and rough quality of the unfinished carving add to its power. 1550–1559 (Galleria dell'Accademia, Florence).

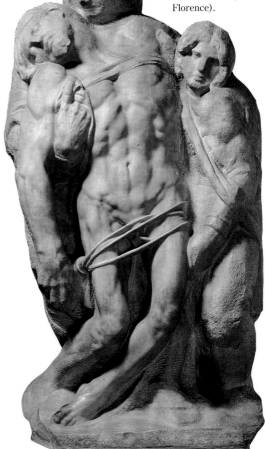

# MICHELANGELO'S LEGACY

Michelangelo enjoyed great fame in his own lifetime. The painter and critic Giorgio Vasari, who wrote the first collection of artist biographies, claimed that Michelangelo's work was perfection. Such a celebrated artist was bound to have imitators. Yet, when younger contemporaries tried to follow in his footsteps, they exaggerated his style, adopting a manner that was pompous and overdone. The name Mannerism came to describe the style of Italian artists in the late sixteenth century. Unlike Renaissance artists, who aimed for naturalism and balance, Mannerists were more interested in artifice and virtuoso technique.

A detail from Vasari's *Cosimo I and the Artists of his Court* (Palazzo Vecchio, Florence).

**♦ FLORENCE AFTER MICHELANGELO**
After Michelangelo's departure for Rome in 1534, Florence witnessed the return of the Medici, who now exercised absolute power. Artists worked mainly in the service of the Medici dukes. When Cosimo I was raised to the rank of Grand Duke, the state of Tuscany became a force to be reckoned with and he wanted the city's art to reflect that. Florentine sculptors tried to duplicate the powerful and heroic aspects of Michelangelo's figures, but their interpretations were often pretentious and lacking in inspiration. Michelangelo was a celebrity in his own lifetime and many artists attempted to imitate his style. Among them were Bartolomeo Ammanati (1511–1592); Bernardo Buontalenti (1536–1608), a pupil of Vasari; and Baccio Bandinelli (1488–1559), a great favorite of the Medici. Both Bandinelli and Benvenuto Cellini (1500–1571) tried to surpass Michelangelo's *David* in the Piazza della Signoria. A Flemish artist, Jean de Boulogne, known as Giambologna (1529–1608), settled in Florence and was also influenced by Michelangelo.

**♦ BANDINELLI**
Baccio Bandinelli was greatly influenced by the work of Michelangelo, imitating his style and eventually becoming a rival. He carved this marble group of *Hercules and Cacus* in 1534 for the Piazza della Signoria in Florence, hoping it would be thought the equal of Michelangelo's *David.*

**♦ CELLINI**
Florentine-born Benvenuto Cellini was a sculptor, goldsmith, and musician. His striking bronze statue of *Perseus,* 1545–1554, shown holding the head of Medusa, was created for the Piazza della Signoria, where Michelangelo's *David* stood. When casting the statue, Cellini is said to have thrown in his pewter household utensils to help the bronze melt and flow.

**AMMANATI ♦**
Bartolomeo Ammanati was another imitator of Michelangelo. His statue of *Neptune,* 1563–1565, which stands above a fountain in the Piazza della Signoria, was unpopular with the Florentines, who nicknamed it "the big white lump." Michelangelo accused Ammanati of ruining a fine piece of marble.

**♦ BUONTALENTI**
An eccentric artist in the service of the Medici, Bernardo Buontalenti was an architect, military engineer, stage and costume designer, and organizer of theatrical extravaganzas. This door for the Uffizi Palace, 1563–1580, with its reversed broken pediment, is one of his most unconventional works.

**NARCISSUS ♦**
Benvenuto Cellini created this figure of *Narcissus*, the beautiful youth who fell in love with his own reflection. 1548 (Museo del Bargello, Florence).

**♦ THE INFLUENCE OF MICHELANGELO**
Baccio Bandinelli created this relief sculpture for the choir of the Florence Cathedral in 1555. Michelangelo's influence on his work is particularly obvious in the powerful muscles and pose of the sleeping nude figure in the center.

**♦ GIAMBOLOGNA**
Giambologna became court sculptor to the Medici. One of his most famous works is this bronze statue of Mercury, the messenger of the gods, which he made for Cosimo I. The foot of Mercury is poised on a puff of wind issuing from the mouth of Zephyr, Greek god of the west wind. 1564–1565 (Museo del Bargello, Florence).

**MICHELANGELO'S ♦ MEMORIAL SERVICE**
After Michelangelo's death, a ceremony was held in the church of San Lorenzo to commemorate him. Cosimo I provided the funds and the church for the occasion, though he didn't attend himself. Right: Agostino Ciampelli, *The Memorial Service of Michelangelo*, 1617 (Casa Buonarroti, Florence).

## MICHELANGELO'S LIFE

Michelangelo returned to sculpture in the final years of his life. He carved three pietàs, returning to a theme that had first attracted him in his youth when he produced the *Pietà* now in the Vatican. The approach of death and his deepening religious convictions seem to have led him to dwell on the subject of Christ's crucifixion. Despite his advanced age, he remained active until the last days of his life. Younger artists who watched him work were astonished at his strength. He continued to work on the dome of St. Peter's, striving to advance his plans as far as possible. Michelangelo died on February 18, 1564, at the age of eighty-eight. His remains were taken to Florence, which he had not seen for thirty years, and were buried in the church of Santa Croce.

# ♦ TIME LINE

| | |
|---|---|
| **1475** | Michelangelo is born on March 6 at Caprese, near Arezzo, second of five sons of Ludovico Buonarroti and Francesca Neri. |
| **1488** | Despite his father's objections, Michelangelo begins an apprenticeship at the workshop of the Florentine painter Domenico Ghirlandaio. |
| **1489** | He leaves Ghirlandaio's workshop to study sculpture at the school set up in the garden of Lorenzo the Magnificent. |
| **1492** | He finishes his relief sculpture *Battle of the Centaurs*. On Lorenzo's death, he leaves the Medici Palace and returns to his father's house. |
| **1494** | Charles VIII of France enters the Italian peninsula. The Medici are expelled and Florence becomes a republic. |
| **1496** | In May, Michelangelo makes his first trip to Rome, where Cardinal Riario becomes his patron. He begins work on his statue of *Bacchus*. |
| **1501** | The Florentine Republic entrusts Michelangelo with an enormous block of marble from which he will create his statue of *David*. |
| **1505** | Pope Julius II commissions Michelangelo to make him a tomb. The ambitious project undergoes many changes over the years. |
| **1508** | After a brief stay in Florence, Michelangelo returns to Rome, where he signs the contract to decorate the ceiling of the Sistine Chapel. |
| **1516** | The new pope, Leo X, a Medici, commissions Michelangelo to design a facade for the church of San Lorenzo in Florence. |
| **1519** | Still employed by Leo X, Michelangelo begins designing the New Sacristy of San Lorenzo, a chapel to house the Medici tombs. |
| **1523** | Leo X's successor, Clement VII, another Medici pope, confirms Michelangelo's commission to work on San Lorenzo. |
| **1527** | The troops of Charles V sack Rome. The Medici are again expelled from Florence. Michelangelo stops work on San Lorenzo. |
| **1529** | Florence is threatened by the armies of Charles V. Michelangelo designs fortifications. The city is besieged and falls in 1530. |
| **1534** | Michelangelo moves permanently to Rome. He resumes work on Julius II's tomb and is asked to paint a wall of the Sistine Chapel. |
| **1536** | Pope Paul III confirms the Sistine Chapel commission and Michelangelo begins work on *The Last Judgment* fresco. |
| **1541** | Michelangelo obtains permission to have Julius II's tomb completed by other sculptors. *The Last Judgment* is complete and unveiled. |
| **1545** | Julius II's tomb is finished, though the version that is finally installed is much reduced from its original design. |
| **1547** | Pope Paul III appoints Michelangelo chief architect of the church of St. Peter's, begun forty years earlier. |
| **1561** | Michelangelo presents the pope with a large wooden model of his design for the dome of St. Peter's. His plans to transform ancient Roman baths into a church are approved. |
| **1564** | Church authorities agree to cover up parts of *The Last Judgment*, on grounds of indecency. Michelangelo dies in Rome on February 18. He is buried in Florence. |

# ♦ GLOSSARY

**allegorical:** having a symbolic meaning

**apprentice:** a beginner who works with a master in order to learn a trade

**autocratic:** having unlimited power

**cameo:** a medallion with an image carved in relief

**contemporaries:** individuals who are living in the same time period

**cornice:** in architecture, a horizontal molding that runs along the top of a wall or just beneath the roof

**Counter-Reformation:** a period beginning in the mid-sixteenth century, with Pope Paul III, during which the Catholic Church responded to the threat of the Protestant Reformation by confirming its basic tenets and instigating some reforms

**dynasty:** A family that maintains power for several generations

**foreshorten:** to shorten the lines of a drawing to create the illusion of depth

**heresy:** In the Roman Catholic Church, a willful denial of the religion's established beliefs

**republic:** a form of government in which citizens elect people to represent them

**translucent:** allowing light to pass through

# WEB SITES

**Michelangelo Buonarroti**
*www.michelangelo.com/buonarroti.html*
An overview of the artist's life.

**The Medici and Renaissance Florence**
*www.pbs.org/empires/medici/index.html*
Explore Michelangelo's city and meet his patrons, the powerful Medici. Includes biographies of Michelangelo and his contemporaries.

**Sistine Chapel Virtual Tour**
*mv.vatican.va/3_EN/pages/CSN/CSN_Main.htm*
Tour the Sistine Chapel. Site includes a map of the ceiling and detailed background informatio

# ♦ LIST OF WORKS INCLUDED IN THIS BOOK

The works reproduced in this book are listed below, with their date, when known, the technique used, their dimensions, the museum or gallery where they are currently held, and the page number. The numbers in bold type refer to the credits on page 64.
Abbreviations:
Works reproduced in their entirety are indicated with the letter E; those of which only a detail is featured are followed by the letter D; MNB, Museo Nazionale del Bargello, Florence.

**ANONYMOUS**
**1** *Bacchus with Satyr*, Roman copy of a Greek original, marble (Museo Chiaramonti, Vatican Museums, Rome) 21 E; **2** *Battle of the Centaurs*, 5th century BC, fragment of marble frieze from the temple of Apollo at Bassae in Arcadia, Greece (British Museum, London) 15 D; **3** *Battle Scene*, 3rd century AD, marble relief on sarcophagus (Museo delle Terme, Rome) 15 D; **4** *Belvedere Apollo*, 2nd century AD, Roman copy of a Greek original, marble, 224 cm (88 in) high (Museo Pio Clementino, Vatican Museums, Rome) 29 E; **5** *The Burning of Savonarola in the Piazza della Signoria*, 1498, tempera on panel, 101 x 115 cm (40 x 45 in) (Museo di San Marco, Florence) 17 E; **6** *Centaur*, 2nd century AD, sardonyx cameo, 5 x 4.2 cm (2 x 2 in) (Museo Nazionale, Naples) 14 E; **7** *Faun*, Roman copy of a Greek original, marble (Museo Pio-Clementino, Vatican Museums, Rome) 21 E; **8** *Florence*, 15th-century miniature, 33.3 x 22.5 cm (13 x 9 in) (from Storia fiorentina dall' Origine della Città fino all'Anno 1455 by Poggio Bracciolini, Vatican Library, Rome) 13 D, **9** *Venus Felix*, Roman copy of a Greek original, marble (Cortile Ottagono, Vatican Museums, Rome) 29 E; **10** *View of the Piazza del Campidoglio*, Rome, 1554-60, etching, 28 x 42 cm (11 x 17 in) (Louvre, Paris) 55 E
**AGESANDER, ATHENODORUS, POLYDORUS**
**11** *Laocoön*, 2nd-1st century BC, marble, 245 cm (96 in) high (Museo Pio-Clementino, Vatican Museums, Rome) 29 E, 30 E
**AMMANATI, BARTOLOMEO**
**12** *Neptune*, 1563-77, marble statue for marble and bronze fountain, 560 cm (220 in) high (Piazza della Signoria, Florence) 60 E
**ANTONELLO DA MESSINA**
**13** *St. Jerome in his Study*, 1474, oil on panel, 46 x 36.5 cm (18 x 14 in) (National Gallery, London) 10 E
**APOLLONIUS OF ATHENS**
**14** *Belvedere Torso*, 1st century BC, marble, 195 cm (77 in) high (Museo Plo-Clementino, Vatican Museums, Rome) 29 E
**BANDIELLI, BACCIO**
**16** *Hercules and Cacus*, 1534, marble, c.496 cm (195 in) high (Piazza della Signoria, Florence) 60 E; **17** Relief with *Sleeping Nude*, 1555 (Museo dell' Opera del Duomo, Florence) 61 E
**BARTOLOMEO, FRA**
**17** *Portrait of Girolamo Savonarola*, early 15th century, oil on panel (Museo di San Marco, Florence) 16 E
**BELLINI, GIOVANNI**
**18** *Dead Christ Supported by the Madonna and St. John*, 1460, tempera on panel, 86 x 107 cm (34 x 42 in) (Brera, Milan) 59 E
**BERTOLDO DI GIOVANNI**
**19** *Apollo*, mid-15th century, bronze, 43.7 cm (17 in) high (MNB) 7 E; **20** *Battle Scene*, mid-15th century, bronze relief, 45 x 99 cm (18 x 39 in) (MNB) 15 E; **21** *Hercules* (attr.), 1470-75, bronze, 49 cm (19 in) high (Victoria and Albert Museum, London) 24 E; **22** *Young Man with Medallion of Plato's "Chariot of the Soul"* (attr.), 1440, bronze bust (MNB) 12 D
**BINK JACOB**
**23** *Joust in the Belvedere Courtyard of the Vatican*, c.1565, etching 57 E
**BOTTICELLI, SANDRO (AND WORKSHOP)**
**24** *Portrait of Young Woman*, 1483, tempera on panel, 82 x 54 cm (32 x 21 in) (Kunstinstitut Gemäldegalerie, Frankfurt) 12 E
**BRONZINO, AGNOLO**
**25** *Holy Family with the Infant St. John* (Holy Family Panciatichi), 1540, oil on panel, 117 x 93 cm (46 x 36 in) (Uffizi, Florence) 31 E; **26** *Portrait of Clement VII*, 1553, oil on metal, 15 x 12 cm (6 x 5 in) (Uffizi, Florence) 33 E
**BRONZINO, AGNOLO (WORKSHOP OF)**
**27** *Portrait of Piero II de Medici*, 1553, oil on metal, 15 x 12 an (6 x 5 in) (Uffizi, Florence) 17 E
**BUONTALENTI, BERNARDO**
**28** Costume sketches for *La Pellegrina*, 1589 (Biblioteca Nazionale, Florence) 50 E; **29** Sketch for a stage-set with buildings in perspective, late 16th century (Uffizi, Florence) 50 E
**CARTARI, VINCENZO**
**30** *Bacchus*, 1556 (from Le Imagine degli Dei Antichi) 20 E
**CELLINI, BENVENUTO**
**31** *Cosimo I*, 1545, bronze bust with traces of gilding, 134.8 x 98 cm (53 x 39 in) (MNB) 48 E; **32** *Narcissus*, 1548, marble, 35 cm (14 in) high (MNB) 61 E; **33** *Perseus*, 1545-54, bronze on marble base, 320 cm (12in) high ( Loggia dei Lanzi, Piazza della Signoria, Florence) 60 E
**CIAMPELLI, AGOSTINO**
**34** *The Memorial Service of Michelangelo*, 1617, oil on canvas (Casa Buonarroti, Florence) 61 E
**COCK, JERONYMUS**
**35** *View of the Piazza del Campidoglio*, Rome, c.1547, etching (British Museum, London) 54 E
**DE GREYSS, BENEDETTO VINCENZO**
**36** *Michelangelo's Bacchus at the Uffizi*, c.1750 (from the Inventario Illustrato della Galleria degli Uffizi) (Uffizi, Florence) 21 E
**DONATELLO (NICCOLÒ DI BETTO BARDI)**
**37** *David*, c.1430-33, bronze, 158 cm (62 in) high (MNB) 25 E; **38** *Madonna and Child* (Piot Madonna) (attr.), c.1460, terracotta with traces of gilding, inlaid with glass, 74 x 75 x 7 cm (29 x 30 x 3 in) (Louvre, Paris) 7 E; **39** *St. George*, 1416-20, marble, 209 an (82 in) high (MNB) 6 E, 26 D
**FERRUCCI, ANDREA**
**40** *Marsilio Ficino*, 1522, bronze bust (Florence Cathedral) 12 E
**FONTEBUONI, ANASTASIO**
**41** *Michelangelo in Conversation with Pope Julius II*, 1620-21 (Casa Buonarroti, Florence) 33 E
**FURINI, FRANCESCO**
**42** *Lorenzo the Magnificent surrounded by artists*, 1636, fresco (Palazzo Pitti, Florence) 10 E
**GHIRLANDAIO, DOMENICO**
**43** Study for *The Marriage of the Virgin*, c. 1485, pen and ink drawing, 20.1 x 26.3 cm (8 x 10 in) (Uffizi, Florence) 8 E
**GIANBOLOGNA (JEAN DE BOULOGNE)**
**44** *Mercury*, 1564-65, bronze, 100 cm (39 in) high (MNB) 61 E
**GIOTTO**
**45** *The Ascension of St. John*, 1315-20, fresco (Santa Croce, Florence) 10 E; 46 Lamentation, 1302-06, fresco (Scrovegni Chapel, Padua) 59 E
**GIULIO ROMANO**
**47** *Aristocratic Banquet*, c.1526, fresco (Venus and Psyche Room, Palazzo del Tè, Mantua) 36 E
**GRANACCI, FRANCESCO**
**48** *Chaties VIII entering Florence*, early 16th century, tempera on panel, 76 x 122 cm (36 x 48 in) (Uffizi, Florence) 16 E
**HAGHE, LOUIS**
**49** *The Church of St. Peter's*, Rome, seen from the Square, 1868 (Victoria and Albert Museum, London) 56 E
**HEEMSKERCK, MARTIN VAN**
**50** *Michelangelo's Bacchus in the Garden of Jacopo Galli*, 1533, etching (Kupferstichkabinett, Berlin) 21 E
**LEVASSEUR, JEAN-CHARLES**
**51** *Michelangelo's Pietà in Florence Cathedral*, 19th century, lithograph, 31 x 24.8 an (12 x 10 in) (Museo di Firenze com'era, Florence) 58 D
**MANTEGNA, ANDREA**
**52** *Bacchanalia with Wine-Vat*, 1470-90, etching, 33.5 x 45.4 cm (13 x 18 in) (Uffizi, Florence) 21 E
**MASACCIO (TOMMASO CASSAI)**
**53** *The Expulsion of Adam and Eve from the Earthly Paradise*, c.1425, fresco, 208 x 88 cm, (82 x 35 in) (Brancacci Chapel, Santa Maria del Carmine, Florence) 11 E; 54 The Tribute Money, c.1425, fresco, 225 x 598 cm (89 x 235 in) (Brancacci Chapel, Santa, Maria del Carmine, Florence) 10 E
**MASOLINO DA PANICALE**
**55** *Adam and Eve bofore their Expulsion*, c.1424, fresco, 208 x 88 cm (82 x 35 in) (Brancacd Chapel, Santa Maria del Carmine, Florence) 11 E
**MELIORE (WORKSHOP OF)**
**56** *Christ Pantocrator*, c.1225, mosaic (Baptistery, Florence) 52 D
**MICHELANGELO BUONARROTI**
**57** *Anatomical study for a human figure*, 1508-12, sanguine, 40.6 x 20.7 cm (16 x 8 in) (British Library, London) 9 E; **58** *Atlas*, 1513-20, marble, 277 cm (109 in) high (Galleria dell'Accademia, Florence) 26 D, 27 E; **59** *Awakening Slave*, 1513-20, marble, 267 cm (105 in) high (Galleria dell' Accademia, Florence) 27 E; **60** *Bacchus*, 1496-97, marble, 184 cm (72 in) high (MNB) 20 E; **61** *Battle of the Centaur*, 1492, marble relief, 84.5 x 90.5 cm (33 x 36 in) (Casa Buonarroti, Florence) 14 E, D; **62** *Bearded Slave*, 1513-20, marble, 263 cm (104 in) high (Galleria dell' Accademia, Florence) 27 E; **63** *Caricature of himself painting the Sistine Ceiling*, 1508-12, pen and ink in the margin of a sonnet written in Rome (Casa Buonarroti, Florence) 37 E; **64** *Ceiling of the Sistine Chapel*, 1508-12, frescos, 13 x 36 in (43 x 118 ft) (Vatican Palaces, Rome) 30 D, 38-39 D, 40 D, 41 D [Caryatid putti 41; The Creation of Adam 38 D; The Delphic Sibyl 30; The Fall and the Expulsion from Eden 39 E; Imitation bronze medallion with The Destruction of the Tribe of Ahab 38 E; The Libyan Sibyl 40; Lunette of Hezekiah, Manasseh, Amon 39 D; Male nudes 41; The Prophet Jeremiah 40; Spandrel above lunette of Jesse, David, Solomon 40 D]; **65** Compositional study for the *Last Judgment*, c.1536, charcoal and sanguine, 41.5 x 29.8 cm (16 x 12 in) (Casa Buonarroti, Florence) 52 E; **66** *David*, 1501-04, marble. 410 cm (161 in) high (Galleria. dell' Accademia, Florence) 24 E, D; **67** *Dying Slave*, c.1513, marble, 229 cm (90 in) high (Louvre, Paris) 35 E; **68** *Florence Pietà*, c.1550-55, marble, 226 cm (89 in) high (Museo dell' Opera del Duomo, Florence) 58 E; **69** *Holy Family with the Infant St. John* (Doni Tondo), c.1506, tempera on panel, 120 cm (47 in) diameter (Uffizi, Florence) 30 E; **70** *Last Judge-ment*, 1536-41, fresco, 13.7 x 12.2 in (45 x 40 ft) (Sistine Chapel, Vatican Palaces, Rome) 52 D, 53 E; **71** *Madonna and Child (Medici Madonna)*, c.1521, marble, 226 cm (89 in) high (New Sacristy, San Lorenzo, Florence) 26 E; **72** Model for the façade of San Lorenzo, Florence, c.1518, wood, 216 x 283 x 50 cm (85 x 111 x 20 in) (Casa Buonarroti, Florence) 43; **73** *Palestrina Pietà*, c.1550-59, marble, 263 cm (104 in) (Galleria dell' Accademia, Florence) 59 E; **74** Plan of bastions for a gate, 1528, pen and brown wash, 29.3 x 41.2 cm (12 x 16 in) (Casa Buonarroti, Florence) 46 E; **75** *Portrait of Andrea Quaratesi*, 1530-40, charcoal, 41.1 x 29.2 cm (16 x 11 in) (British Museum, London) 8 E; **76** *Rebel Slave*, c.1513, marble, 215 cm (85 in) high (Louvre, Paris) 35 E; **77** *Rondanini Pietà*, 1552-64, marble, 195 cm (77 in) high (Castello Sforzesco, Milan) 26 D, 58 E; **78** Sketches of blocks for the façade of San Lorenzo, Florence, 1521, pen, 20.4 x 30.3 cm (8 x 12 in) (Casa Buonarroti, Florence) 34 E; **79** *St. Peter*, copied from Masaccio's Tribute Money, c.1490, pen and sanguine on white paper, 39.5 x 19.7 cm (16 x 8 in) (Graphische Sammlungen, Munich) 10 E; **80** Study of the *Belvedere Apollo*, sanguine (Louvre, Paris) 28 E; **81** Study for a door at the head of the staircase of the Laurentian Library, Florence, 1526, charcoal; pen and wash, 40.5 x 25.3 cm. (16 x 10 in) (Casa Buonarroti, Florence) 6 E; **82** Study for a Pietà, 1533, charcoal, 25.4 x 31.8 cm (10 x 13 in) (Louvre, Paris) 58 E; **83** Study for the arm of *David*, 1501-04, pen on paper, 26.5 x 18.7 cm (10 x 7 in) (Louvre, Paris) 25 E; **84** Study for the *Tomb of Pope Julius II*, 1513, charcoal, pen and wash, fragment, 29 x 36.1 cm (11 x 14 in) (Uffizi, Florence) 35 E; **85** *Tomb of Giuliano de' Medici*, Duke of Nemours, 1524-34, marble, 6.3 x 4.2 in (21 x 14 ft) (New Sacristy, San Lorenzo, Florence) 44 D, 45 D; **86** *Tomb of Lorenzo de' Medici*, Duke of Urbino, 1524-34, marble, 6.3 x 4.2 in (21 x 14 ft) (New Sacristy, San Lorenzo, Florence) 44 D, 45 E; **87** *Tomb of Pope Julius II*, 1512-45, marble, 7 x 6.9 in (23 x 23 ft) (San Pietro in Vincoli, Rome) 35 E; **88** Two male figures, copy of Giotto's *Ascension of St. John*, c.1490, pen on white paper, 31.7 x 20.4 cm (12 x 8 in) (Louvre, Paris) 10 E; **89** *Young Slave*, 1513-20, marble, 256 cm (101 in) high (Galleria dell' Accademia, Florence) 27 E; **90** *Vatican Pietà*, 1498-15M, marble, 174 cm (69 in) high (St. Peter's, Rome) 26 D, 59 E
**MICHELOZZO (WORKSHOP OF)**
**91** *Tondo with Centaur*, 15th century, relief (courtyard of Palazzo Medici Riccardi, Florence) 14 E
**PALMA VECCHIO (JACOPO NEGRETTI)**
**92** *Holy Family with the Infant St. John and Mary Magdalene*, 1508-12, oil on panel, 87 x 117 cm (34 x 46 in) (Uffizi, Florence) 31 E
**PIERO DI COSIMO**
**93** *Battle of Lapiths and Centaurs*, late 15th century, oil on panel, 71 x 260 cm (28 x 102 in) (National Gallery, London) 15 E
**POCCETTI, BERNARDINO**
**94** *Cosimo I instituting the Accademia del Disegno*, early 17th century, fresco (Loggiato degli Innocenti, Florence) 49 E; **95** *Pier Capponi tearing up the Agreement with Charles VIII*, 1583-86, fresco (Reception Room, Palazzo Capponi, Florence) 17 E
**POLLAIUOLO, ANTONIO**
**96** *Niccolò Machiavelli*, late 15th century, marble bust (MNB) 23 E
**RAPHAEL**
**97** *Portrait of Angelo Doni*, 1506, oil on panel, 63 x 45 cin (25 x 18 in) (Galleria Palatina, Palazzo Pitti, Florence) 30 E; **98** *Portrait of Maddalena Strozzi*, 1506, oil on panel, 63 x 45 cm (25 x 18 in) (Galleria Palatina, Palazzo Pitti, Florence) 30 E; **99** *Portrait of* Julius II, 1512, tempera on panel, 108.5 x 80 cin (43 x 31 in) (Uffizi, Florence) 32 E; **100** *Portrait of Leo X with Cardinals Luigi de' Rossi and Giulio de' Medici*, 1518, tempera on panel, 155.5 x 119.5 cm (61 x 47 in) (Uffizi, Florence) 32 D; **101** *The School of Athens*, 1508-11, fresco (Stanza della Segnatura, Vatican Palaces, Rome) 32-33 E, 32 D
**RAPHAEL (WORKSHOP OF)**
**102** Grotesque decoration for the Stufetta (bathroom) of Cardinal Bibbiena, 1516, fresco paintings (Vatican Palaces, Rome) 36
**ROSSELLI, MATTEO**
**103** *Michelangelo as Commissioner for Fortifications*, 1615, oil on canvas (Casa Buonarroti, Florence) 47 E
**ROSSELLINO, BERNARDO**
**104** *Tomb of Leonardo Bruni*, 1446-50, partly gilded marble, 7.2 m (23 ft) high (Santa Croce, Florence) 19 D
**SANSOVINO, JACOPO**
**105** *Bacchus with Satyr*, c.1514, marble, 146 cm (57 in) high (MNB) 20 E
**SEBASTIANO DEL PIOMBO (SEBASTIANO LUCINI)**
**106** *Portrait of Vittoria Colonna*, c.1535, oil on panel, 69 x 54 cm (27 x 21 in) (Museo di Palazzo Venezia, Rome) 50 E
**SIGNORELLI, LUCA**
**107** *Holy Family*, 1490-91, tempera on panel, 124 cm (49 in) diameter (Uffizi, Florence) 31 E
**TITIAN**
**108** *The Emperor Charles V of Habsburg on Horseback*, 1548, oil on canvas, 3.3 x 2.8 m (11 x 9 ft) (Prado, Madrid) 47 D; **109** *Portrait of Pope Paul III with his nephews Cardinals Alessandro and Ottavio Farnese*, 1546, oil on canvas, 210 x 174 cm (82 x 69 in) (Galleria Nazionale, Naples) 33 D
**TRIBOLO, NICCOLÒ**
**110** *Fiesole*, allegorical statue for a fountain at the Medici Villa,Castello, Florence, early 16th century, marble (MNB) 19 E
**UTENS, GIUSTO**
**111** *Medici Villa*, Poggio a Caiano, late 16th century, tempera on canvas, 143 x 285 cm (56 x 112 in) (Museo di Firenze com'era, Florence) 19E 19E
**VASARI, GIORGIO**
**112** *The Arrival of Leo X in Florence*, 1555-62, fresco (Leo X apartment, Palazzo Vecchio, Florence) 25 E; **113** *Cosimo I and the Artists of his Court*, 1555-62, fresco (Palazzo Vecchio, Florence) 50 E, 60 D; **114** *Portrait of Lorenzo de' Medici*, 1488-90, oil on panel, 90 x.72 cm (35 x 28 in) (Uffizi, Florence) 10 E; **115** *The Siege of Florence*, 1555-62, fresco (Leo X apartment, Palazzo Vecchio, Florence) 47 E
**VERROCCHIO, BYNAME (ANDREA DI CIONE)**
**116** *David*, before 1476, bronze, 126 cm (50 in) high (MNB) 25 E; **117** *Female head*, second half of 15th century, metal point, white and grey highlights on paper prepared with an orange ground, 26.7 x 22.5 cm (11 x 9 in) (Louvre, Paris) 8 E; **118** *Putto with a Dolphin*, c.1476, bronze, 67 cm (26 in) high (Palazzo Vecchio, Florence) 7 E

# ♦ INDEX

# ♦ CREDITS

The original and previously unpublished illustrations in this book may be reproduced only with the prior permission of Donati Giudici Associati, who hold the copyright. Abbreviatons: t, top; b, bottom; c, center; l, left; r, right.

**ILLUSTRATIONS**
Simone Boni, pp. 8-9, 11, 22-23, 28-29, 48-49, 50-51; L.R. Galante. pp.16-17, 34-35, 36-37, 46-47, 56-57; Simone Boni - L.R. Galante, pp. 4-5; Simone Boni - Francesco Petracchi ,pp. 54-55; Andrea Ricciardi, pp. 42-43; Sergui, pp. 6-7, 12-13.
COVER: Simone Boni
TITLE PAGE: L.R. Galante

**WORKS OF ART REPRODUCED**
Alinari, Florence: 29, 70, 77; Alinari/Giraudon: 18, 47, 67, 80, 90; Biblioteca Nazionale, Florence: 28; Bridgeman Art Library, London: 2,24, 49, 75; British Library, London: 57; British Museum, London: 35; Casa Buonarroti, Florence: 63, 65, 72, 74, 78; DoGi: 3, 33, 101; DoGi/Serge Domingie, Marco Rabatti: 5, 12, 15, 16, 17, 19, 20, 22, 23, 25, 26, 27, 30, 31, 34, 36, 37, 40, 42, 43, 48, 50, 51, 54, 58, 59, 60, 61, 62, 66, 68, 69, 71, 73, 84, 85, 86, 89, 91, 95, 97, 98, 100, 108, 112, 113,114, 115, 116, 118; DoGi/Mario Quattrone: 46, 52, 53, 55, 104; Serge Domingie, Marco Rabatti, Florence: 32, 39, 41, 81, 87, 92, 94, 96, 99, 103, 105, 107, 110, 111, 113; Graphische Sammlungen, Munich: 79; Eric Lessing, Vienna: 109; Museo di Palazzo Venezia, Rome: 106; Museo Nazionale, Naples: 6; National Gallery, London: 13, 93; Franco Cosimo Panini, Milan: 56; RMN: 10, 38, 76, 82, 83, 88, 117; Scala, Florence: 4, 9, 11, 102; Vatican Museums, Rome: 1, 7, 8, 14, 64; Victoria and Albert Museum, London: 21.

**PHOTOGRAPHS**
Achim Bednorz: p. 54b; DoGi: pp. 18c, 49, 57b; DoGi/Serge Dominige, Marco Rabatti: pp. 18tl, 18-19, 32, 42tr, 42cl, 43t; DoGi/Mario Quattrone: p. 18bl; Serge Domingie, Marco Rabatti, Florence: p. 42c; Liberto Perugi: 61tl.